HOW TO RENOUNCE YOUR US CITIZENSHIP IN TWO EASY STEPS

BY **GLEN LEE ROBERTS**
'EARTHLING'

T0101984

A SPECIAL LIMITED EDITION

Glen Lee Roberts

NIMBLE
WISDOM

ISBN 978-99953-2-895-5

TABLE OF CONTENTS

FINAL STATEMENT
Written Statement Relative to Renunciation

I think at the first moment of looking at a blank screen to begin writing this, the thought came to mind that this is "supposed" to be some kind of in-depth, angry, rant about all the real and/or perceived "injustices" of the United States at a personal as well as global level. I also believe that had I sat down ten years ago to write this, that is probably what would have resulted.

However, my decision to renounce my US citizenship is not based on a need to "condemn" the United States; it is rather based on how I have changed over the past years – in particular, during the almost 11 years that I have lived outside the United States.

When I think about going to the US consulate to renounce my US citizenship, it reminds me of my trips to the Colombian Consulate for my divorce. I was moving out of a relationship that provided some degree of comfort and security, but no longer provided that "spark of life," as it once did. I also felt a tinge of anxiety about what the future would bring apart from my (then) wife. However, I was also confident that I would look back and see it was the right decision. And, at this time, I can see that clearly that it was.

Take a quick look at Glen Roberts, below. I've set my US passports from 2002 and 2007 side-by-side. I say "quick look" because quite simply, I don't like the person you see in the 2002 photo! I believe you will see a profound difference between the two, as I do.

This process also brings to mind a memory from much further in my past as well: In particular, the meeting scheduled today for the consular official to explain the implications renouncing US citizenship (something I have researched and considered for a number of years already). I believe the meeting today will be conducted in a completely professional manner and with respect for my decision. However, it reminds of when the high school I attended became aware that I wasn't going to complete their program. The phrase they used of course, was "drop out."

They met with me, to explain the implications of "dropping out." I don't believe that meeting was held in a professional nor respectful manner and was simply to degrade me for my decision. Though possibly a difficult decision (or at least unpopular), I also look back on that as being a decision, that in the end was profoundly beneficial for me.

As I said above, I have lived outside the United States for nearly eleven years. Additionally, the last time I visited the United States was in February of 2003. For me, the United States is a "foreign country." The first insight into how I have changed during that time is the difference in my passport photos. However, I believe that I have changed much more profoundly than is reflected by the photos. I would say that physically, emotionally, mentally and spiritually I am not the same person.

I have contemplated and researched the implications regarding the renunciation of my US citizenship for a number of years. Of course, there was nothing preventing me from renouncing in 2010, 2011, 2012 or any year since 2002. Except, it wasn't right for me at those times.

Now, I have come to the point where I believe it is the right choice for me. And, just like my experience with other difficult decisions in my life, I am confident that in a few years I will look back and see it was the right decision for me and made at the right time.

Glen Lee Roberts
June 11, 2013

INTRODUCTION

Hello, as a newly arrived earthling (legally speaking anyway), I'm writing this book for other earthlings who wish to renounce their US citizenship in favor of another country or in favor of *not* having any citizenship.

In this book, you'll find information pertaining to my own story about renunciation and also resources you'll find useful if you choose to go down this path. There are numerous attachments toward the back of this book: government forms that you will need to know about.

Generally, I've tried to put together a useful compendium of information with a personal perspective that makes what might seem intimidating a little more personal and less formidable. There are many myths out there about what this process is like; I've tried to address them in order to remove whatever "fear factor" may be present.

These days, having a citizenship can be difficult. If you are from the US, for instance, you have apply for a visa to go to certain countries. Brazil, for instance, instituted a visa policy for US citizens as retaliation for US insistence that Brazilians needed to apply for a visa. Obtaining a visa may not look like much of an inconvenience, but it comes with additional cost not only in money but also in time.

A little background on this issue … Did you know the entire passport/visa system is only about 75 years old? In the 1800s, gentlemen for the most part traveled where they liked in the world and a passport was considered something of an affront.

Both the passport system and the international criminal agency Interpol were initiated early in the 20th century but World War I and the subsequent Depression put off their general adoption. Only after World War II did the passport system and Interpol become more aggressively implemented. Now almost every day, somewhere in the world, it's being elaborated on.

There's no doubt that the system is time-intensive and a growing impediment to the free-flow of travel. None of this is historically unusual. Countries throughout the ages have often had internal passports – travel restrictions that required citizens to obtain "papers" before traveling around the country.

These sorts of restrictions tend to be cyclical, as a matter of fact. Unfortunately, such cycles can take hundreds of years to resolve themselves, and in the meantime if one is born in a particular era, one must deal with such restrictions as one can. Taking a historical view is recommended but not to the exclusion of taking action to retain as much of one's personal freedoms as possible.

In the US, particularly, such restrictions have never been implemented but if current trends hold, the passport system that is in force country-to-country may expand until it involves internal applications. Unfortunately, the US is now leading the way when it comes to some of these applications, including a "no fly" list that continues to expand and may already include hundreds of thousands – and will eventually include millions. Once you are on such a list, it's very difficult to get off.

Somehow the state now sees its position as one that allows it to determine your travel-worthiness whether you have overtly committed offense or not. This is a kind of "pre-crime" approach to law-enforcement and one that in the end depreciates our human value while denying us due process.

We are of biological origin. We are of the Earth and in my view, we should make our allegiances to the Earth and not self-declared "leaders" prejudging us and making decisions about what we can think, what we can do, what we can say, where we can go and how we can get there.

Now let me add the following: It's not my intention to make this book a polemic about what's going on in the West and particularly in the United States when it comes to increased travel restrictions and to the shrinking of everyday freedoms in general.

But for any thinking person – and people who are contemplating international travel are usually among such individuals – the trends should be obvious. Such trends, by the way, are driven by a number of factors and are not usually reversed. In fact, the drivers usually become even more powerful over time.

As an Earthling – Your Life, Your Values

This report is based on my own personal experiences. After living outside the USA for 11 years, I didn't feel that I belonged there. I didn't feel people had the right idea about me when they discovered I was "American." Over time, I found myself less able to "relate" to Americans, particularly the culture and politics.

By choosing to be "stateless," I chose to be self confident. I rejected the concept that my worthiness was tied up in the state's evaluation of whom I was. My involuntary allegiance to a group of leaders or others was not going to define my self-worth or my living or lifestyle options.

Of course, in creating a personal value system, one should try not to adopt a philosophy that involves engaging in activities which may harm or disrespect others; however, one should also be aware that "states" constructed of the many anonymous servants of leviathan, often make decisions that are harmful.

These decisions may benefit a small clique of elite leaders. Just as surely, they may depreciate either militarily or economically, regions and living standards of those who for one reason or another are seen as impediments to the goals of those exercising state power.

In 1996, the US implemented a legal policy of what some call "naming and shaming" so-called renunciants. It is sad Americans consider it shameful for other citizens to exercise their legal rights. No one who has (or will) appear on the federal register list should feel ashamed, nor should anyone reading the list use that label.

Should you become stateless? There is no requirement that you hold another nationality to renounce your US citizenship. Many people insist that it is required. As proof that it is not, I have included in this book a copy of my Certificate of Loss of Nationality of the United States (CLN) and you can see that I held no other nationality at the time I renounced (nor now, 15 months later as I write this, do I have any nationality at all).

The US Consul did give me a printout from the Foreign Affairs Manual (FAM), the State Department's Operational manual for the embassies with some details on the challenges of being stateless (included in a documents section below). It is an option available; however, I would recommend you seriously study of the topic ahead of time.

Some like to use the phrase, "citizen of the world" to refer to a stateless person, particularly one that made the voluntary choice to become one. I was never quite comfortable with that as it implies that one needs an allegiance with, or subservience to something.

The issue of taxes in the United States is one that is overly complicated, and the renunciation of US citizenship has its own unique and complicated tax issues. That is a topic which you should seek professional assistance on and evaluate the available options for assistance carefully.

The actual renunciation process does not involve any tax issues or questions. Whether you are "compliant" or not at the time of your renunciation does not affect anything.

You will often see the phrase "covered expatriate" when reading topics that address the issue of taxes and loss of citizenship. A covered expatriate is simply a person who has assets above a certain amount, or hasn't fulfilled various tax obligations for the past five years. The "covered expatriate" has to file a more complicated tax return, and may have additional tax liabilities, but with a $668,000 exemption.

If you are not wealthy, if you don't own a home or stocks, it may well be that the only difference being a "covered expatriate" means is additional paperwork during the year you renounce. If you believe that phrase may refer to your situation, then it warrants more research on your tax situation.

Changing 'Homeland'

The complexity of the tax code along with the ruinous over-printing of money by the Federal Reserve are examples of how "these united States" have changed from the intention of the founding fathers.

I believe if one steps back and looks at the United States, its policies, laws, media, and behavior are much different than "original intention." A new system is being ushered in, one that has uncomfortable similarities to those of enemy states that the US fought in World War II and later in the Cold War.

The media and politicians distract us with emotional issues of little true relevance and dash our hopes by providing a choice between two equally unsatisfactory options. The result is an ever increasing level of fear, anger and overall dissatisfaction.

The discontentment in return calls for or encourages oppressive political policies so that we can be kept safe. The media is there fanning the fire, and gradually our freedoms and quality-of-life degrades. All the while, we are congratulating ourselves on how much better we are than everyone else because of our great historical documents.

Nowhere within the system are we provided a means or opportunity to sit back and consider the situation. Regretful of the past, afraid of the future, we are left with no possibility of finding peace within ourselves.

When I was engaged in my activities as a "privacy activist," (independent publisher) my activities probably resulted in little more than making people angry and afraid. They didn't help resolve the issues. I regret that now. I've spent a lot of time since then thinking about ways I could make a more satisfactory contribution.

A few days ago the thought popped into my mind: "Books are ideas on paper. People are ideas in action." There are, after all, a lot of good books with some great ideas. Yet, like the Declaration of Independence of the United States or the Bill of Rights – those ideas have little importance or meaning, if they are not brought into action.

We can revere such ideas all we want, but they have no meaning until you and I put them into action; a task that seems insurmountable in many cases.

In the past, I have tried to put my ideas on paper as an independent news media owner, one publishing newsletters, reports, articles, and radio broadcasting, all attacking the injustices of the system (as I saw them). Yet, I never brought those ideas into action in a viable way.

Recently we've seen Edward Snowden expose injustices of the United States. In fact it was something I had researched about 30 years ago. However, even with all his exposure, nothing has changed. The NSA is still spying and the politicians are still convinced it is necessary.

In fact, it is even worse than that. The deep security state offers us riddles inside of secrets – and some have argued that Snowden's revelations accommodated the NSA. Various officials, the argument goes, wanted to let the world know of the agency's capabilities but didn't want to issue a press release for obvious reasons.

Snowden, by advertising the capabilities of the NSA, addressed that difficulty. Everyone knows about the NSA now – how it is spying and what it has done to make its programs truly universal. For the public, it has brought out more fear, anger and discontentment. Yet, what are the opportunities for "hope and change?"

Around the world, it seems that all the systems are basically the same. They are just at different places in their cycles. Since I have now stepped outside the system, I am no longer supporting it on a physical, emotional, mental or spiritual level. Those systems of course impose various limitations on me because of their rules and regulations, etc. However, at least I am not directly bound by (involuntary) allegiances and fidelities.

I realize that I will always be at a disadvantage when dealing with any "organized" system. My goal, simply put, is to live in mutual respect with occupants (people, plants, animals) of our planet, and even the planet itself.

I realize too that is something much easier said than done, though I hope to set an example by putting my ideas into action in a way not achieved socio-politically or economically by most … and in a way that causes someone to stop for a moment and ponder the situation; in a way that does not fan the fires of fear and anger.

Why Renounce Your Citizenship?

While it seems that a large portion of the world's population wants to move to the United States and become a citizen there, there is a movement of another kind too.

As throughout the history of the United States, some American's chose to leave the country and renounce their citizenship. That process based on my personal experiences is straightforward and simple.

One aspect of the process that is completely irrelevant is the question "Why?" It is simply your right to renounce, and the choice is yours alone to make. But as a practical matter, everyone that learns of your decision will ask you why! For me, the short answer is simply *that I outgrew the United States.*

The long answer would start with something along the lines of: "For roughly 20 years, basically my entire adult life in the United States I was in conflict. My conflict was with every nature of 'authority', local, state, corporate, prestigious universities as well as at a federal level including the CIA, the FBI, the US military and even the President of the United States."

The conflict was a result of my independent journalism and perspectives on privacy, surveillance, freedom of information and related topics. Really, it was my so-called protected First Amendment activities, ie: expression of my viewpoints on those topics which was the conflict.

In the past decade, I've tried to resolve some of the emotional conflicts I experienced. For me, part of this process included renouncing citizenship.

I was speaking with a Paraguayan about translating my Certificate of Loss of Nationality (CLN) to Spanish (an official translation). At first he only briefly glanced at the document, but as our conversation drifted on, he looked at the document and then remarked, "This is a really an important document isn't it?"

I responded, "yes," and then we discussed the topic in depth. He asked if I considered myself a "libertarian." I responded that I didn't like to use labels, but that would certainly be a better label than "republican" or "democrat."

As our conversation was coming to a close, he said, "I can't believe I asked if you were a libertarian, I see clearly you are an Earthling." That is exactly it. I am made of the elements of the Earth and when my time here is over, I will return to the Earth.

This introduction has covered some basic issues pertaining to citizenship and statelessness. In the next sections, I'll discuss my own background in a little more detail and then explore specifically the "two steps" necessary to withdraw your citizenship.

1

MY STORY

I have lived outside the USA since late 2002, and my last visit to the USA was in February of 2003. I could have renounced any time since then. I could look back and say, "I should have renounced March 1, 2003". In some ways that would have been a good idea.

However, I was a much different person then. I probably would have written an angry rant to go along with my renunciation. I probably would have had a huge hassle with the consulate staff going in with an attitude of "the USA is full of ----" and I'm gonna "show them". I wasn't out of the US mindset either, so life would have been very difficult for me.

I do have some grand stories. In the mid-1980s as an early Internet buff, I became interested in how the 'Net was going to change our lives and affect our privacy. As an object lesson, I published some public information from government officials – and this received the predictable reaction (actually more of a reaction than I'd expected). Articles were written and top US officials responded, sometimes angrily.

An ex-marine general quoted in the Wall Street Journal even stated that I "needed to worry less about privacy and more about being hit upside the head with a closed fist."

The counsel to then-President Ronald Reagan had a file in his office titled: "Glen Roberts vs. Foreign Intelligence Surveillance" (dated 1985).

Yes, in 1985 the President was apparently interested in me because I was interested in the FISC (the same thing Snowden blew the whistle on). In Dec. of 1999, The Pittsburgh Post Gazette published an article saying that, "[unnamed] members of the military... said Roberts was becoming a threat to national security."

I eventually moved abroad (as you can imagine) but last year I realized that I still hadn't done enough. I'd outgrown the US, yet was still carrying around the baggage I'd accumulated from my education, and criticisms regarding government policies, actions, technology the Internet.

I'd researched the topic of renunciation over the years and now, with determination to act, I did a quick review. The only way to make an appointment at the US Embassy in Asunción, Paraguay (where I lived) was via the online system.

You have two choices: 1) Notary Services; and 2) Other. I chose "other" and made an appointment. The day before my appointment I decided to email and let them know the reason for my visit. The response from Maria G. Ramirez was prompt, but a bit disappointing:

I am glad you wrote us about your appointment for renouncement as I am in charge of American Citizen Services and will be out on a training this week's afternoons. The person covering me has probably never done a renunciation before. Do you think we can reschedule you for next week?

I requested that she make an appointment for me as soon as possible.

One of the optional parts of the process is to submit a statement about why you are renouncing. It can be written or oral. I think if you plan to provide a statement, a written one would be best.

I don't believe it has any impact on the results, unless maybe it would give them doubt as to your voluntariness or intention. Also, if for some reason you felt the need to threaten officials, they would make a report to the Secret Service. Remember, once you have renounced, you are no longer American and have no need to fret over politics or anything else in that country.

My original plan was to forgo any statement. However, at the last moment, I sat down to write a Statement Relative to Renunciation (you should have already read that). The words easily flowed; the whole purpose of my renunciation was about me, and not the United States.

Writing the statement was cathartic and I experienced a rush of emotions pertaining to how I'd arrived at this moment. I "re-lived" what I'd been through, which is sort of what you are supposed to do when you are dying. I suppose it was a kind of mini-death – leading to rebirth! If not physically, spiritually.

I recalled how I long ago began to explore possibilities of living at least part of the time outside of the US. Although I spent a few months in Europe as a teenager, my life outside the United States really started in 2002. I took a long weekend in Costa Rica. That trip was difficult, but I experienced life away from the stresses of the United States.

I did some better planning and made another trip later that year. And that opened the door, even though I really wasn't thinking about moving yet. Then I made plans for a one month trip. I left in December, 2002.

During that trip, I rented a house and returned to the United States to pick up a few things. I returned to Costa Rica in February 2003, and haven't been to the United States since. When I moved into my house in Costa Rica, I was thinking that I'd adopt a lifestyle of a month or two in Costa Rica and then a month or two in the United States.

That never happened, because as I began to de-stress from a steady diet of politics, divide-and-conquer news and economic and political fear-mongering, I started to feel much better. You could say I rediscovered what it felt like to be a normal human again. Or at least I was able to perceive that the possibility existed.

The time I spent in Costa Rica, though, was fraught with issues; I knew I wanted to emigrate but I just hadn't found the right place.

In June of 2005, I moved to Uruguay. The plan was to go and check it out to see if we – me and my then-wife – liked it. At that time there was no information for expats seeking to live in Uruguay. I think it's better that way, to start an adventure with a completely open mind.

I stayed in Uruguay until early 2011 when I relocated to Paraguay where I reside now. A short trip to Asunción, "sold" me on the advantages of Paraguay over Uruguay.

I am writing from where I live in Asunción and I have to say I've never been happier. The choices I've made after a good deal of deliberation have proven to be, so far, the right ones for me. Since you are reading this book, I hope it helps clarify some of the issues that you may be struggling with.

Leaving the country of your birth is never easy, but as we will see in upcoming chapters, much of the anxiety surrounding this decision can be lessened by absorbing the proper information.

2

GETTING STARTED

There are plenty of people with no personal experience offering opinions online. I don't see how they can provide any useful information. However, they are of course entitled to their opinions and to share them.

Here is one example. Below are a few excerpts and my comments from, *"Loss of nationality: How to lose your citizenship. by Andrew Henderson | Dec 18, 2013"*

(http://nomadcapitalist.com/2013/12/18/loss-of-nationality-how-to-lose-your-citizenship/).

I should note that this is just a blog that I randomly happened across. It is one of many examples of where I feel the issue is being overshadowed with unnecessary emotion.

"Citizens of the United States and most other countries have a hard time simply canceling their own citizenship."

In my experience it was surprisingly simple and pleasant.

"Countries don't want to allow their citizens to become stateless, allegedly because they believe they'd still be on the hook for said former citizen should no other country take him or her in. If you don't believe me, try walking into any US Embassy with no second passport and telling them you want to renounce your US citizenship."

I did exactly that.

"They'll likely tell you you're barking mad."

I can't speak for what they thought of me (nor is it important). But they certainly didn't tell me anything close to that. All of my interactions with the staff and consulate officials were professional and pleasant. I even had a nice conversation with the US Consul about issues not related to the process at all (my trips to the Amazon, his time as US Consul in Bolivia).

Recently, I've seen many press reports talking about the price increase and suggesting that one seeking to renounce must go through two "intensive interviews" ... something that leads people to feel that maybe they are taking a trip to Guantanamo Bay, not exercising a fundamental right.

I think after reading this report you'll better understand the process and what to expect. As there are many US Consulates around the world, you can be sure that there will be differences. However, they are all following the same guide and I believe they will be professional.

That said, I am sure they are fully aware of FACTA, as well as all the real and perceived injustices of the United States, ie: they've heard it all. Remember, bringing those kinds of topics up isn't a part of the renunciation process.

The process is about you. It is not about them. There is no need to enrage yourself, nor tire out the embassy staff with the repetition of all the political complaints that abound in todays world. The truth is renunciation is your escape from it. You are putting the United States and all their problems behind you. You are closing the door on them and needn't look back.

The process itself is enough of a political statement that there is no need to enunciate anything more.

Renunciation vs. Relinquishment

This report deals with the process of renunciation. There is a similar process of relinquishment.

The paperwork is similar; in fact the Certificate of Loss of Nationality (CLN) is the identical document. In my case they had me complete the relinquishment paperwork as well (that caught me off guard).

Of course, the renunciation process is just performing the "expatriating act" in front of a consular officer, ie: taking the Oath. My recommendation is that even if you performed an "expatriating act" with the intention of losing US citizenship, it is a better idea to simply renounce.

The reason is simple. The consular officer has to make a decision: Did you intentionally and voluntarily give up your citizenship? With the renunciation process, you attend a "renunciation ceremony." You appear before him (or her) and take an Oath. In normal circumstances there is no question in his mind what your intention was.

Renunciation: loss of US citizenship by voluntarily "renouncing" in front of a consular officer, outside the United States. In some cases this could be done inside the US during time of war, but that is beyond the scope of this report.

Relinquishment: loss of US citizenship by performing an "expatriating act" with the intention of losing US citizenship. The bottom line is the key. Renunciation has a definitive result: loss of citizenship. Relinquishment may get you there too, but is it full of obstacles.

When I completed my renunciation on June 21, 2013, the fee was US$450. Apparently there was no fee for relinquishment at that time. They have since raised the fee to US$2,350. I'm not sure if there is a fee for relinquishment. By comparison, I recently read that Jamaica charges US$1,000 for citizens to renounce. The renunciation process is not one that necessitates a lawyer.

3

TWO EASY STEPS

Step 1: The Interview

The first meeting is referred to as the "interview." I arrived at the consulate a little bit early and was immediately taken through security. In Asunción, there is an outside waiting area before the security checkpoint.

When I arrived at the consulate, I was promptly called to the window and was presented with copies of several forms to complete: DS-4079, DS-4080, and DS-4083. Yes, they asked me to complete the "certificate of loss of nationality" as well as the relinquishment form.

They said the latter might have some useful information. I had tried to complete a copy of all the forms ahead of time, but that one caught me off guard. Keep that in mind, even if your plan is to follow the renunciation procedure you may be well advised to fill out the DS-4079 just in case.

COPIES OF ALL THESE documents are included in the documents section below as I filled them out.

After completing the forms, I presented them, as well as my old (canceled) US passport and my then-current US passport. My old canceled passport was handed back to me. "We don't need that."

I was asked to take a seat. After a short while I was called back to the window and told, "he [the US Consul] needs your old passport." I asked, "because of my letter?" There was a little smile or giggle as I handed over my old passport. I returned to my seat.

The wait wasn't long before I was called to the window by the US Consul, David Schensted. I was greeted with something to the effect of, "*I see that life in MERCOSUR has been good to you*". (MERCOSUR is a regional alliance of some South American countries.)

Not even close to being aggressive or confrontational as I had imagined. Nor did it fit with Andrew Henderson's suggestions that, it would be difficult or you'd be called insane if you didn't hold another nationality.

We had a brief conversation about life in South America, my trips to Peru and his time as US Consul in Bolivia. There wasn't an inkling of negativity; in fact, he was completely neutral and accepting of my decision.

He then explained that he had to read me the **Statement of Consequences of Renunciation** (Form **DS-4081**). You can review that statement ahead of time so you can be fully prepared for your "interview." I've included a copy of all these forms in the documents section.

Because I would become stateless, he gave me a photo copy of a page out of the FAM on that topic. We also had a brief discussion of that, but mostly relative to my travel with my Paraguayan ID instead of my US passport and how that might relate to the Vienna Convention.

He said I could make another appointment in a week for the "Renunciation Ceremony" and that it would be quick. Everything would be ready for me. I would just need to sign it and that would be it. I suggested that Maria G. Ramirez, again, make the appointment for me and she agreed. The second appointment was about 10 days later. They refer to it as the "Renunciation Ceremony."

Step 2: The Ceremony

Again, I arrived early and immediately passed through security and to the consulate. I checked in at the window and was asked to take a seat. This time, I can't use the word prompt. My waiting time was probably close to two hours.

Everyone was serviced ahead of me and then I was alone in the room waiting. Two tests of their emergency system were conducted. First a *duck and cover,* followed by an *evacuation.* Loud sirens, followed by loud firm instructions and of course a note that it was just a test and not to actually do anything.

Duck and cover is a method of personal protection against the near prompt effects of a nuclear explosion. It is useful in conferring a degree of protection to practitioners outside the radius of the nuclear fireball but still within sufficient range that by standing upright death or serious injury is certain.

As a countermeasure to the lethal effects of nuclear explosions, it is effective in the event of both a surprise nuclear attack, which might come at any time without warning, and in the more likely event of sufficient warning of a few seconds to minutes being given, but not enough advance notice to permit an effective evacuation.

[http://en.wikipedia.org/wiki/Duck_and_cover]

Those who feel the US has a bad attitude towards people renouncing their citizenship might feel that was some kind of subtle intimidation. It was more likely just a coincidence. Either way it was an interesting experience.

I was then called to the cashier and paid the required US$450 fee. Incidentally, at least at the Consulate in Asunción, Visa and Mastercard are accepted. After paying the fee I returned to my seat.

Not long thereafter, I was called to the window. This time by Joel Fifield, the Vice Consul. Everything was right down to business. He started reviewing the documents and everything looked good. Then he paused and I thought uh oh, there's a problem!

Well, there was a problem, but it wasn't a big deal. He said that he knew that David Schensted had already read me the Statement of Consequences of Renunciation (Form DS-4081) the week before, but that he had to sign that he had personally read it to me. So, he read it to me.

Then he passed the **Oath/Affirmation of Renunciation of Nationality of United States** (Form DS-4080) to me and told me to raise my right hand and read it and upon completion sign it. I completed the oath and signed the form. In effect at the moment I was no longer a US Citizen!

I signed two copies of the Oath and several other documents. Joel Fifield did his signing and asked me to take a seat. After a short wait, I was called to the window and presented with an original signed and sealed Certificate of Loss of Nationality of the United States, and my previously current US Passport canceled.

That day, June 21, 2013, I had walked into the US Embassy an American citizen and walked out without any nationality, Stateless: an Earthling.

4

THE WAITING GAME

Although the CLN I received on June 21, 2013 immediately after my renunciation ceremony was signed and sealed by an officer of the United States, they claim it is not actually valid until "approved" by Washington. David Schensted had told me that process takes a couple weeks and they are never rejected.

Of course as a practical matter, rejecting an application after an officer of the United States signs and sealed it would be a bit odd. It would leave me with a certificate anyone in the world would on its' face accept as valid. In my case that couple of weeks turned out to be nearly 15 months.

I emailed Maria G. Ramirez every couple of months to check on the status of things. The "excuse" was always the same, that there was a backlog in Washington and they didn't assign much staff to handle the workload. According to her the main problem was a flood of renunciations, mostly in Europe due to FACTA.

One expat I know mentioned that he was going in to renounce and tell them all about the evils of FACTA because "they need to know". Or something like that. I think it is clear they already know.

There are a number of practical issues with respect to the significant delay. The renunciation is effective on the day of the Oath, not the date of approval. So, as of June 21, 2013, I was not a US citizen, but it wasn't "approved" until Sept 2, 2014!

On September 15, 2014, Maria G. Ramirez, sent me email stating that I had been approved and asking me to bring in my CLN to have it stamped. I made an informal appointment to stop by the next day. This time I had to wait in the outside waiting area for a short time before security let me in.

However, once in the consulate, I was promptly called to the window, ahead of two others that were already there waiting for service. The stamp was quickly applied to my CLN and I was on my way.

Although the process of renunciation of US citizenship inherently carries a strong political statement, the actual process is simply bureaucratic. There is no need to express any anger about US policies, nor to anticipate any kind of poor treatment.

I believe the staff of the US Consulates are professionals and will treat you in a professional manner and do their job as trained, be it a passport renewal or a citizenship renunciation. For that I would like to thank, US Consul David Schensted, Vice Consul Joel Fifield, and Maria G. Ramirez head of American Citizen Services, as well as the rest of the staff that worked on my case.

At the back of this book, I have reproduced a copy of all the documents relating to my case. You can use these for reference about the kind of information you will need to provide. I was told the **Request for Determination of Possible Loss of United States Citizenship** (Form DS-4079) didn't need to be very detailed. If, however, you are choosing the relinquishment route, I would consider it important to be quite detailed there.

I have included the written statement I provided. For me, the most important aspect of this, and of my time living outside the USA, is the shift that occurred – from focusing on certain anger issues pertaining to the US to focusing on ways I could become more physically and emotionally healthy.

I think much of that shift came by simply being away from the daily stresses of life in the US – the noxious political noise, the fear mongering media (TV, radio and websites). Another big part of the shift in my attitudes came, I believe, from the time I spent deep in the Amazon rain forest. That story, though, has to wait for another day.

If you decide to provide a written statement, please don't copy mine. Write your own. Write it from your heart. The bottom line is that renouncing your U.S. Citizenship is your right, it is your choice. The process is straight forward and quite simple. You needn't share your decision with anyone outside the Consulate nor worry that you will be hassled by the staff of the Consulate in anyway.

5

CONCLUSION

The process of renouncing your US citizenship is not actually intimidating or complex, as I've attempted to show; actually it's "quick and easy". It is also your right. You and only you can make the decision of whether to go ahead with it.

In most of the news reports and many of the websites I've read on the topic, the details get buried in the emotions, especially anger. The fact is that it is a simple process that involved some pretty simple and straightforward paperwork.

If you've made the decision to renounce, then as it is popularly said, *just do it*. Remember, though however, quick and easy the process actually is, it is a very important decision and the effect is irreversible.

For myself, I've felt lighter. Some friends have even asked if I am losing weight. The burden of carrying around the weight of being an "American" and all that might entail is suddenly gone. I can focus on what I believe is important in my life without the burdens of any involuntary allegiances.

You will be able to walk into a US Embassy as an American and leave as a "foreigner." With one signature, you can step outside of all the politics and drama. You will be reborn, ready to experience the world as whatever other nationality(ies) you have, or as in my case without any nationality at all.

The key to it all is the Oath. The essential part of that Oath says:

"I desire and hereby make a formal renunciation of my US nationality, as provided by section 349(a)(5) of the Immigration and Nationality Act of 1952, as amended, and pursuant thereto, I hereby absolutely and entirely renounce my United States nationality together with all rights and privileges and all duties and allegiance and fidelity thereunto pertaining. I make this renunciation intentionally, voluntarily, and of my own free will, free of any duress or undue influence."

Remember, *all rights and privileges and all duties and allegiance* you had as an American are gone. Of course the IRS will require you to file an excessively complicated return for the year you renounce. However, after that you will be treated like any other foreigner, ie: taxed only on your US Source income, if any.

Within this book you'll find a copy of the relevant parts of the **Foreign Affairs Manual** (FAM) from the US State Department regarding renunciation. Some of that relates to the process and some contains a good overview of the history of citizenship renunciation in the United States.

Remember, that is a government manual. It seems to have little if anything that would discourage an American from renouncing their citizenship, nor to inspire fear or anger about the process.

Also included are some basic thoughts on citizenship and renunciation. I've intermixed a few comments in that based on my experiences.

If you decide to renounce your US citizenship, I wish you well with the process and your new life. If you chose not to, or not to at this time, I'll share the words from an old friend when she heard of my renunciation:

"No club worth its salt would try to keep people from leaving. Sorry to lose you though."

6

ADDENDA: RESOURCES AND CHECKLIST

Here are some tips on how you can search for additional information if you wish. And, most importantly, how to limit those searches to specific websites or departments of the US government. Google offers a very good method for restricting searches. Here are some examples:

nationality site:.gov

(The site:.gov has no spaces it in). This will provide a listing of all .gov wesbites with the term nationality in it. Sometimes Google will do a broader search, so:

"nationality" site:.gov

Will list only websites with the exact word, nationality and be a .gov site. For the topic of renouncing your nationality, site:.gov is really too board. There are probably there departments you'll be interested in researching:

site:state.gov (U.S. State Department)
site:justice.gov (U.S. Justice Department)
site:irs.gov (Internal Revenue Service)

Depending on your circumstances or interests you might also consider:

site:ssa.gov (Social Security Administration)
site:.mil (U.S. military sites)

site:federalregister.gov (The Federal Register)
(for example to find the Quarterly list of people who have expatriated: "Required by Section 6039G" site:federalregister.gov) Other searches could turn up agency regulations.

site:un.org (United Nations)
site:unhcr.org (United Nations Refugee Agency)
site:ohchr.org (United Nations Office of the High Commissioner for Human Rights)

You might want to search other sites, groups or agencies and can simply use site: to restrict your search to their website.

Some of the phrases you may wish to use in your searches could be:

"loss of nationality"
"voluntary renunciation"
"renounce citizenship"
"certificate of loss of nationality"

You may consider doing the same search using the word "nationality" and "citizenship" to see how the results may change. Use your imagination. Of course you can do searches without the site: and search the entire web.

You can also use the search feature directly available on the agency sites, however, you may find that Google has a broader index of their website(s).

Also, to locate the latest copies of the relevant State Department Forms, I would recommend using:

DS4083 pdf site:state.gov
DS4081 pdf site:state.gov
DS4080 pdf site:state.gov
DS4079 pdf site:state.gov

This website will help you locate US Embassies and Consulates around the world: http://www.usembassy.gov/

Renunciation Check List

□ Make the decision. If that decision including becoming Stateless, I would recommend doing some serious research on the topic ahead of time.

□ Consult with a tax professional to be clear on what your filing requirements will be in the year you expatriate in, as well as any obligations relative to tax deferred accounts and US source income in future years.

□ Select which consulate (embassy) you will expatriate at. If you have another citizenship and passport, you may wish to shop around for one that doesn't have a significant scheduling backlog.

□ Schedule your appointment. If you are forced to do this via an online system and cannot clearly identify the purpose of your visit, I would contact the **American Citizen Services** section to be sure someone will be able to handle your expatriation needs at the time and date you selected. Inquire as to the method for paying the fee (ie: cash, credit card, or deposit in a bank ahead of time).

□ Printout and complete these State Department forms:

- **DS-4083 (Certificate of Loss of Nationality of the United States)**. Complete the information you are able to, ie: your basic information, other nationalities (if any), etc.

- **DS-4081 (Statement of Understanding Concerning the Consequences and Ramifications of Renunciation or Relinquishment of US citizenship)**. Your name is about all this one needs. It is the statement that will be read to you during your "interview".

- **DS-4080 (Oath / Affirmation of Renunciation of Nationality of United States)**. Your name, date and place of birth, last address in the USA and a bit more if you were Naturalized.

- **DS-4079 (Request for Determination of Possible Loss of United States citizenship)**. The FAM says that this form is not usually used in renunciation cases, but could provide some "useful" information. In my case the consulate asked for it and I was caught off guard. I would recommend completing it at home, so if it is requested you don't have to waste time completing it at the consulate.

- **DO NOT SIGN ANY OF THE FORMS.**

☐ On the day of your appointments, arrive early with a pleasant attitude and plenty of patience. The renunciation process is strictly related to paperwork. At the first visit they read you a "warning" (ie: Form **DS-4081**). At the second visit you take an Oath (ie: Form **DS-4080**). That's it. You are out of the system and can get on with your live and leave all the U.S. emotional baggage in the past.

☐ Remember to take your US passport (or other proof of being a US Citizen if you don't have a current passport) and the above listed documents. After your first interview your passport will be returned to you. After you take the Oath of Renunciation, your passport will either be destroyed, or canceled and returned to you.

☐ If you have another nationality it would be a good idea to take along proof of that (passport, naturalization certificate, etc). If you don't have another nationality, it would be a good idea to bring along proof that you are legally resident in the place you are.

☐ The renunciation fee will be collected at the second meeting, the "Renunciation Ceremony", before you take the Oath. Be sure you know the required procedure to pay the fee. It is not refundable.

7

FURTHER ADDENDA:
CORRESPONDENCE WITH MICHIGAN STATE
REGARDING BIRTH CERTIFICATE

The Right to Change Nationality vs. Your Birth Certificate

Section 15 of the "**Universal Declaration Of Human Rights**" says: "Everyone has the right to a nationality. No one shall be arbitrarily deprived of his nationality *nor denied the right to change his nationality.*" (my emphasis added).

I believe there are issues at a state and local level that are an infringement on the individual right to change one's identity to a non-US Citizen.

At the Federal level, the US State Department cancels one's passport, issues a **Certificate of Loss of Nationality of the United States** and notifies a number of other federal agencies of your loss of nationality, in specific Homeland Security, the FBI, and the IRS.

The issue arising with respect to birth certificates is outside the confines of the federal government. My birth certificated was issued by the State of Michigan, and in any moment that I need a copy, that state stands ready to issue a certified copy for my benefit.

In recent correspondence, T.B. Weaver, Deputy State Registrar, Vital Records & Health Data Services Section, explained the role of the state with respect to birth certificates: *"The role of vital records office is to accurately record the facts at the time of an individual's birth."*

I believe that is exactly right, a birth certificate records a person's birth. The Michigan birth certificate makes no mention of nationality or anything of that nature.

However, I believe the most common use of a birth certificate is not to prove you were born, but to prove you are a US citizen. Even the "US Citizen and Immigration Services" of Homeland Security says, *"Your birth certificate provides proof of citizenship"*.

A quick review of other websites finds the same. The Michigan Secretary of State uses your birth certificate as proof you are legally in the US when applying for a driver's license. South Carolina uses it as proof you are a US citizen when enrolling at the state university. California uses it as a proof when you enroll in some health care plans. The list of state and local agencies using birth certificates as "U.S. Citizenship Certificates" is simply endless.

However, in reality, a birth certificate issued in the United States can at best prove that an individual under age 18 is a US citizen. All US citizens over the age of 18 have the right to renounce their citizenship. However, those who make the choice to exercise that right are forever burdened with a birth certificate that in effect falsely declares them to be a US citizen.

The door is open for criminals, ie: identity thieves, and/or illegal aliens to seek out the birth certificates of those who have given up their US nationality. The likelihood of the real holder of that birth certificate making a complaint is low.

In the past criminals sought out birth certificates of people who had passed away to use for obtaining false ID. That activity apparently became so widespread that birth certificates are now updated to reflect when a person has died. As you can see from the correspondence below, T.B. Weaver, rejected my request that my birth certificate be updated to reflect that I am not a US citizen.

So, in effect, Michigan insists on issuing a certificate that for all practical purposes is a "Certificate of U.S. Citizenship" in my name! This is a clear violation of my rights: If I changed my nationality, why would I wish to be falsely labeled a citizen after my renunciation? If I changed my nationality why would the State of Michigan issue a de facto Certificate of Citizenship on my behalf?

I do agree that it would be not be viable, nor appropriate to update one's birth certificate whenever nationality changes. In many cases it is completely irrelevant. Say you are a dual citizen, US and French. There would be no need to note the French citizenship on the US birth certificate.

However, upon the loss of US citizenship, regardless of what other nationalities may be held by that person, the birth certificate becomes in conflict with itself and the truth; it becomes false! It clearly labels a non US citizen as a US citizen. One cannot effectively renounce his citizenship if the authorities at any level continue to declare that person a citizen.

In many ways, the loss of US nationality is similar to "death". For example, the Internal Revenue Service says: *"as if he or she had died on the day before the expatriation date as a citizen or resident of the United States"* (Internal Revenue Bulletin: 2009-45: **Guidance for Expatriates Under Section 877A).**

If the Internal Revenue Service views renunciation as "death," I think it would be difficult to understate the significance of loss of nationality of the United States.

Loss of citizenship is not a reversible action. Once lost, an individual may not change his mind and have citizenship reinstated. One would have to go through the entire citizenship process, just as if one were an alien – which indeed one would be.

The issue, I believe is even more significant outside the United States. When an individual born in the US is required to provide a birth certificate, that document may be viewed as a "Certificate of U.S. Citizenship" by foreign authorities, in the same manner it is by State and local authorities within the US. This might well stymie an effective "change of nationality."

Below are copies of emails between myself and the State of Michigan. I first emailed the Michigan Department of Community Health, and after about a week, having heard nothing, I emailed a State Representative there.

I recently received a reply to my email from the Department of Health. All three emails are reproduced below (in chronological order. I have removed the email address).

From: Sr. Glen
Sent: Friday, September 19, 2014 2:04 PM
To: Grijalva, Nancy (DCH)
Subject: Birth Certificate Issue

I am writing to you today to express concern with respect to Birth Certificates issued by the State of Michigan.

I was born in Washtenaw County and have previously contacted the Country Clerk there and he said he was in contact with the State and was not able to address my issue.

As I am sure you are aware, a Birth Certificate issued by a State within the USA is considered "proof" of citizenship. Both within the United States, and I believe around the world as well.

For example, the U.S. Federal Agency, "US Citizen and Immigration Services" of "Homeland Security" says:

Are you a citizen born in the United States? Your birth certificate provides proof of citizenship. If you need a copy of your birth certificate, contact the Bureau of Vital Statistics in the State in which you were born. We do not issue any kind of citizenship document to a person who is a citizen by birth in the United States." http://www.uscis.gov/us-

Therein, lies the problem. I was born in Washtenaw County, Michigan, yet *I am not a citizen of the United States.* I had contacted the County Clerk to see if my Birth Certificate could be amended in some way to reflect my non-US citizen status, rather than its current misrepresentative form.

The answer he apparently received from the State, was that the death of a person could be added to their birth certificate, but not other amendments related to the "status" of the person could be made. The notation of death, I believe is done to prevent fraud.

The lack of a clear indication of lack of US citizenship on a state-issued document that is taken for granted as proof of citizenship, I believe, could lead to similar types of fraud and other issues. For example, the type of person who in the past would look for the birth certificate of a person who had passed away, may now look for the birth certificate of one who is not a citizen (lists of those people's names are published in the Federal Register regularly). The key element being that a non-citizen is unlikely to be residing within the USA and therefore much like a "dead person" for the purposes of one who might seek to commit fraud.

Additionally, the non-citizen, if was present in the USA could use their birth certificate to misrepresentation their own nationality for work and/or other purposes.

Outside the United States when the person is required to provide a birth certificate, it will likely be incorrectly interpreted as proof of "US citizenship" for a person who is not a US citizen.

It is difficult to locate statistics, however, I believe there are approximately 24,000 individuals who may have US birth certificates and are not US Citizens. With a simple average we might conclude approximately 500 may have Michigan birth certificates.

That number may not be large, but one would hope that the State of Michigan would not provide official records that do not provide an accurate description of the person.

I realize that the U.S. State Department does not appear to notify State's or County Clerks when a person loses their US citizenship and therefore it may be difficult to know about or record the change. However, I think it would be appropriate the States to have an system to allow such a notation to me made on a case by case basis. For example, an additional check box on your already existing form used to make changes or corrections of name, parents, etc.

In that respect, I hereby include a copy of my "Certificate of Loss of Nationality of the United States" and request that my birth certificate be updated to reflect my status as a non-Citizen of the United States. I am sure the U.S. State Department in Washington, or the U.S. Consulate in Asunción, Paraguay can verify the authenticity of the attached document if needed.

Sincerely,
Glen Lee Roberts
Asunción, Paraguay

From: Sr. Glen
Date: Fri, Sep 19, 2014 at 5:43 PM
Subject: Problem with State of Michigan, re: Birth Certificate
To: Jeff Irwin [Michigan House of Representatives]

I am writing to you from Asunción, Paraguay. I am not a Citizen nor resident of the United States. However, I have an issue with the State of Michigan and hope you will give it due consideration.

I was born in Ann Arbor, Michigan. That means that I have a Birth Certificate issued by the State of Michigan. Unfortunately, that Birth Certificate is used by most authorities within and without the United States as "proof of citizenship".

I contacted the County Clerk in Washtenaw County to see if my Birth Certificate could be appropriately noted so while it would indicate I was born there, that I was not a Citizen of the United States. He contacted State Officials and was informed that no such notation is possible.

The result being that I feel the State of Michigan's Vital Records are mis-representative of the real situation in my case (and that of others born in Michigan who are not Citizens of the United States). I have contacted the State and included a copy of my email to them below. I won't repeat here the specifics I've included in that letter.

A good part of my concern is the fact that, in fact, I have no nationality at all. In some parts of the world, I believe that type of situation is fairly common. However, in the region of the world where I live now, it is quite unknown. I am concerned that there could be some authorities who could be uncomfortable with my situation may use my birth certificate to apply or continue to use an incorrect label of "American Citizen" with respect to me. For example, a financial institution when presented with a Certificate from the consulate that I was not a US citizen, entered my nationality as "American Citizen" in their computer system regardless.

In fact, I believe anyone who viewed my Birth Certificate as it exists now would probably apply the same label to me, and rightfully so, based on the information contained within the document, and the common use of Birth Certificates as "proof of citizenship". However, it is it not a correct, nor appropriate label.

As a Stateless person, I understand that my "standing" within the legal and political systems of the world may be quite limited. At best, I have a small number of United National conventions available for my protection (notably, none of which is the United States a party to). Therefore, it is extraordinarily important that the State of Michigan not issue document(s) that would misrepresent my status, as my birth certificate does at this time.

As I am sure you are aware, the United Nations, Universal Declaration of Human Rights, Article 15, section 2 provides: "No one shall be arbitrarily deprived of his nationality *nor denied the right to change his nationality*". I exercised my right to change my nationality, in accordance with that right and the Nationality Laws of the United States as administered by the U.S. State Department.

I now ask that the State of Michigan respect my exercise of that right. I look forward to whatever assistance you can provide and have included my letter to the State of Michigan below.

Sincerely,
Glen Lee Roberts
Asunción,   Paraguay

From: Weaver, Tamara (DCH)
Date: Tue, Sep 30, 2014 at 10:25 AM
Subject: FW: Director's Office Assignment - Log #09191404
To: Sr. Glen
Cc: "Reinhart, Denise (DCH)" [Secretary, Bureau of Family, Maternal and Child Health] "Danieli, Sharon (DCH)" [Secretary, Director's Office, Constituent Inquiries], "Anderson, Paula (DCH)" [Secretary, Public Health Administration]

Mr. Roberts,

I have read through your concerns and do believe that you have drawn some accurate conclusions. Based on the stated policies of some federal agencies which accept evidence of birth in the United States as proof of citizenship, there will be times when the assumptions behind such a policy are wrong.

A vital records office is not positioned to address the problem you have outlined.

The role of vital records office is to accurately record the facts at the time of an individual's birth. Each state establishes the facts to be recorded for each birth in their state. Michigan and nearly all other states design their certificates of birth by following nationally developed standard forms. Citizenship is not a specific standardized item on U.S, standard certificates. More information on those forms is available through the internet at: http://www.cdc.gov/nchs/nvss/

Recording citizenship on an original birth certificate would not be appropriate. A determination of citizenship for a newborn by a physician, hospital staff or a public health worker would not have any legal significance even if recorded on the birth certificate. Official citizenship determinations are reserved for the federal government while vital records registration is governed by the states.

A citizenship status recorded at the time of birth could not be relied upon over time. The citizenship status of someone can change but a birth certificate would not. Birth certificates are prepared at the time of birth and are then held to document the facts at that point in time. A birth certificate is not changed when the facts at the time of birth change, such as when someone changes residence or adopts a new name. This would be true of citizenship status as well.

I am sorry that the vital records office is in no position to help you address/resolve your concerns.

I would suggest that you raise these issues directly with the federal agencies who have adopted policies that can result in the types of error you have highlighted.

Regards,
T.B. Weaver
Deputy State Registrar
Vital Records & Health Data Services Section
Division for Vital Records and Health Statistics
201 Townsend, 3rd Floor
Lansing, MI 48933
(517) 335-9748 (voice)
(517) 335-9264 (fax)

8

DOCUMENT APPENDIXES

Below I have reprinted the actual documents that were used in my voluntary renunciation of U.S. Citizenship. They are presented in the order of the State Department Form number. This is all there is to it!

As stated a number of times within the text of the book, the most complicated form here is the DS-4079 and that is not usually used in renunciation cases. You can download the blank forms from the State Department Website. http://www.state.gov (see my resource section for details on how to locate the forms).

You can then complete them at home and arrive at the consulate completely prepared.

I have also included two pages that the U.S. Consul printed from the FAM regarding being stateless.

Following the document reprints, is a copy of the State Department's Foreign Affairs Manual (FAM) as it relates to loss of citizenship issues. While reviewing that if the process starting feeling overwhelming, simply refer back to the actual forms that are required to help bring it into perspective.

U. S. Department of State

BUREAU OF CONSULAR AFFAIRS

OMB NO. 1405-0178
EXPIRES: 12/31/2013
Estimated Burden -15 minutes

REQUEST FOR DETERMINATION OF POSSIBLE LOSS OF UNITED STATES CITIZENSHIP

The following information is needed to determine your present citizenship status and possible loss of U.S. citizenship. You cannot lose U.S. citizenship unless you VOLUNTARILY perform an act designated by U.S. statute and do so with the intent to relinquish U.S. citizenship. You are advised to consult an attorney before completing this form. If you have any questions about the form, you should discuss them with a member of our consular staff before completing the form. You are requested to complete this form carefully. Use extra paper as needed and attach any supporting documents to this form.

PART I

1. Name (Last, First, MI)			2. Date of Birth (mm-dd-yyyy)	3. Place of Birth
Roberts	Glen	L	05-05-1962	Ann Albor, Michigan USA

4. (a) Last U.S. Passport Number	(b) Issued at (Place)	(c) Issued on (Date) (mm-dd-yyyy)
426678401	U.S. Deparment of State	07-02-2007

5. If not born in the United States, did you acquire citizenship by birth outside the United States to U.S. citizen parent(s) [ ] Yes [ ] No or Naturalization? (Naturalization petitions prior to 11/29/1990 were submitted to and adjudicated by a court. After that date they were submitted to and adjudicated by INS/USCIS.) [ ] Yes [ ] No

(a) Name of Naturalizing Court/Office _____ (b) Date of Naturalization (mm-dd-yyyy) _____

Dates and Countries of Residence Outside the United States Since Birth

Date (From) (mm-dd-yyyy)	Date (To) (mm-dd-yyyy)	Country
12-01-2002	05-01-2005	Costa Rica
05-01-2005	02-01-2011	Uruguay
02-01-2011		Paraguay

6. When did you first become aware that you might be a United States citizen (Give Approximate Date)?

Born in USA

7. How did you find out that you are a citizen of the United States? (For example, did you always know you were a U.S citizen? If not, when did you learn about your citizenship? Did someone tell you that you are a U.S. citizen?)

Always knew or parents told me

8. Legal Resident of Uruguay and Paraguay

8. Are you a national or citizen of any other country other than the United States? [ ] Yes [X] No

(a) If yes, of what country? _____

(b) If yes, did you acquire that citizenship in the foreign country by:

(i) Birth? [ ] Yes [ ] No

(ii) Marriage? [ ] Yes [ ] No

(iii) Naturalization or registration; if yes, please provide a date (mm-dd-yyyy) _____ [ ] Yes [ ] No

DS-4079 (Formerly FS-581) 12-2011   (If more space is needed, use additional paper)   Page 1 of 5

(c) If other, explain

(d) If you checked YES to question 8 (B) part (iii) by what means, or in what kind of proceeding, were you naturalized as a citizen of a foreign state?

9. Have you taken an oath or made an affirmation or other formal declaration of allegiance to a foreign state? ☐ Yes ☒ No

If yes, please provide a date *(mm-dd-yyyy)* and country _____

(a) If you checked YES to question 8 or 9 or both, what was the nature of the oath you took? What were the words used? If you have a copy of the oath please attach it

10. Have you served in the armed forces of a foreign state? ☐ Yes ☒ No

(a) If so, what country? _____

(b) In which branch of the armed forces did you serve? _____

(c) Dates of Service *(mm-dd-yyyy)* _____

(d) What ranks did you hold? _____

(e) What was your highest rank? _____

(f) What responsibilities did you have and what functions and activities were you engaged in?

(g) Did you take an oath? If so, describe the oath ☐ Yes ☒ No

11. Have you accepted, served in, or performed the duties of any office, post or employment with the government of a foreign state? ☐ Yes ☒ No

(a) If yes, please provide dates of service, country and the job title

(b) What were your duties and responsibilities for each of the foreign government jobs you held?

(c) Did you take an oath, affirmation, declaration or allegiance in connection with the job? If yes, describe the oath, affirmation, declaration or allegiance. ☐ Yes ☒ No

12. What ties did you have to the country where you performed the act or acts indicated in Questions 8-11? For example:

(a) Did you maintain a residence? If yes, please explain. ☒ Yes ☐ No

I own a residence in Paraguay

(b) Did you own property? If yes, please explain. ☒ Yes ☐ No

Yes

(c) Do you have family or social ties? If yes, please explain. ☒ Yes ☐ No

I have social ties in Uruguay and Paraguay as I have spent significant time in each

(d) Do you vote? If yes, please explain. ☐ Yes ☒ No

(e) What other ties did you have to the country where you performed the act or acts indicated in Questions 8-11?

I have permanent legal residence in both Paraguay and Uruguay

13. What ties do you retain with the United States? For example:

(a) Do you maintain a residence? If yes, please explain. ☐ Yes ☒ No

(b) Do you own property? If yes, please explain. ☐ Yes ☒ No

(c) Do you have family or social ties? If yes, please explain. ☒ Yes ☐ No

My parents and brother, sister, live in the USA

(d) Do you vote? If yes, please explain. ☐ Yes ☒ No

(e) Do you file U.S. income or other tax returns? If yes, please explain. ☒ Yes ☐ No

Form 1040 + attachments

(f) Do you maintain a profession, occupation, or license in the United States? If yes, please explain ☐ Yes ☒ No

(g) Have you registered your children as citizens of the United States? ☐ Yes ☒ No

14. What passport do you use to travel to and from the United States?

Have not been to USA since Feb 2000. Used U.S passport

15. What passport do you use to travel to and from other countries?

I use my Uruguay and/or Paraguay Cedula

16. Have you renounced your U.S. nationality at a U.S. Consulate or Embassy? If yes, provide a date and place ☐ Yes ☒ No

It is my intention to do so now

17. Describe in detail the circumstances under which you performed the act or acts indicated in Questions 8-16.

I arrived at the Consulate on June 11, 2013, for the initial interview and was given this form to complete

18. Did you perform the act or acts voluntarily? ☒ Yes ☐ No

(a) If not, in what sense was your performance of the act or acts involuntary?

(b) Did you perform the acts with the intent to relinquish U.S. citizenship? If so, please explain your answer ☒ Yes ☐ No

19. Did you know that by performing the act described in Questions 8-18 you might lose U.S. citizenship? Please explain your answer

Yes. My intention is to renounce my U.S. Citizenship

20. Your answers on this form will become part of the official record in your case. Before signing this form, you are advised to consider consulting with an attorney, and to read over your answers to make certain that they are as complete and accurate as possible. If you would like to provide additional information you believe relevant to a determination of your citizenship status, and in particular to your intention or lack of intention to relinquish U.S. citizenship, you may attach separate sheets with that information.

If your answer to each of the questions above is "No," please sign below before a Consular Officer at a U.S. Embassy or Consulate. If you answered "Yes", to one or more of questions 8(b)(iii)-11 and your action was completely VOLUNTARY, please continue with PART II.

Subscribed and Sworn

[SEAL]

Signature

Signature of Consular Officer

Vice Consul

DS-4079 (If more space is needed, use additional paper) Page 4 of 5

21. You should be aware that under United States law, a citizen may lose U.S. citizenship if he/she voluntarily performs any of the acts specified above in questions 8(b)(iii)-11 with the intent of relinquishing United States citizenship. If you voluntarily performed an act stated above with the intent to relinquish United States citizenship, you may sign Part II of this statement before a Consular Officer at a U.S. Embassy or Consulate. The U.S. Consulate or Embassy will prepare the forms necessary to document your loss of U.S. citizenship.

PART II

STATEMENT OF VOLUNTARY RELINQUISHMENT OF U.S. CITIZENSHIP

Subscribed and Sworn

I, _____ Glen Lee Roberts _____, performed the act of expatriation indicated in Questions 8-19

voluntarily and with the intent to relinquish my U.S. citizenship.

Signature

Date (mm-dd-yyyy) 06/21/2013

[SEAL]

Signature of Consular Officer

Date (mm-dd-yyyy) 06/21/2013

Joel A. Fifield
Vice Consul
of
The United States of America

PRIVACY ACT STATEMENT

AUTHORITIES: The information on this form is requested under the authority of 8 U.S.C. 1104, 1481, 1483, 1488, and 1501, and 22 U.S.C. 212. Although furnishing the information is voluntary, applicants may not be eligible for a U.S. passport or for relinquishment or renunciation of U.S. nationality if they do not provide the required information.

PURPOSE: The principal purpose of gathering this information is to determine if the individual performed a potentially expatriating act as defined in 8 U.S.C. 1481 voluntarily and with the intention of relinquishing U.S. nationality.

ROUTINE USES: The information solicited on this form may be made available to foreign government agencies to fulfill passport control and immigration duties, to investigate or prosecute violations of law, or when a request for information is made pursuant to customary international practice. In the event a finding of loss of nationality is made, the information solicited on this form may be made available to other federal entities with law enforcement responsibilities relating to or affected by nationality, including but not limited to the U.S. Citizenship and Immigration Service, the Internal Revenue Service, and the Federal Bureau of Investigation. The information provided also may be released to federal, state or local agencies for law enforcement, counter-terrorism and homeland security purposes; to Congress and courts within their sphere of jurisdiction; and to other federal agencies for certain personnel and records management matters.

Paperwork Reduction Act (PRA) Statement

Public reporting burden for this collection of information is estimated to average 15 minutes per response, including time required for searching existing data sources, gathering the necessary documentation, providing the information and/or documents required, and reviewing the final collection. You do not have to supply this information unless this collection displays a currently valid OMB control number. If you have comments on the accuracy of this burden estimate and/or recommendations for reducing it, please send them to: A/GIS/DIR, Room 2400 SA-22, U.S. Department of State, Washington, DC 20522-2202.

U. S. Department of State

BUREAU OF CONSULAR AFFAIRS

OATH/AFFIRMATION OF RENUNCIATION OF NATIONALITY OF UNITED STATES

Asuncion
(Embassy/Consulate)   at

Paraguay
(Country)   ss

I, Glen Lee Roberts , a national of the United States
Name _(Print Full Name)_

solemnly swear/affirm that I was born at Ann Arbor
(City or Town)

Washtenaw County , Michigan , on 05-05-1962
(Province or County)   _(State or Country)_   Date _(mm-dd-yyyy)_

That I formerly resided in the United States at:

166 Plum St
(Street Address)

Oil City, PA 16301
(City, State and ZIP Code)

That I am a national of the United States by virtue of:

[X] Birth in United States or Abroad to U.S. Parent(s)

[ ] Naturalization   Date of Naturalization _____
Date _(mm-dd-yyyy)_

(If naturalized, give the name and place of the court in the United States before which naturalization was granted.)

(Name of Court)

(Street Address)

(City, State and ZIP Code)

I desire and hereby make a formal renunciation of my U.S. nationality, as provided by section 349(a)(5) of the Immigration and Nationality Act of 1952, as amended, and pursuant thereto, I hereby absolutely and entirely renounce my United States nationality together with all rights and privileges and all duties and allegiance and fidelity thereunto pertaining. I make this renunciation intentionally, voluntarily, and of my own free will, free of any duress or undue influence.

(Signature)

Subscribed and sworn/affirmed to before me this 21 day of June , 2013

at the Asuncion Consulate   Paraguay
(Embassy/Consulate)   _(Place)_

(Signature of Officer)

SEAL   Joel Fifield
(Typed Name of Officer)

Vice Consul of the U.S.A
(Title of Officer)

Note: A renunciation of United States nationality/citizenship is effective only upon approval by the U.S. Department of State but, when approved, the loss of nationality/citizenship occurs as of the date the above Oath/Affirmation was taken.

DS-4080
01-2013   Page 1 of 1

U. S. Department of State
Bureau of Consular Affairs

STATEMENT OF UNDERSTANDING CONCERNING THE CONSEQUENCES AND RAMIFICATIONS OF RENUNCIATION OR RELINQUISHMENT OF U.S. CITIZENSHIP

I, _____ Glen Lee Roberts _____ , understand that:

1. I have the right to renounce/relinquish my United States citizenship.

2. I have the intention of relinquishing my United States citizenship.

3. I am exercising my right of renunciation/relinquishment freely and voluntarily without force, compulsion or undue influence placed upon me by any person.

4. Upon renouncing/relinquishing my U.S. citizenship, I will become an alien with respect to the United States, subject to all laws and procedures of the United States regarding entry and control of aliens.

5. If I do not possess the nationality/citizenship of any country other than the United States, upon my renunciation/relinquishment I will become a stateless person and may face extreme difficulties traveling internationally and entering most countries and maintaining a place to reside.

6. If I am found to be deportable by a foreign country, my renunciation/relinquishment may not prevent my involuntary return to the United States.

7. My renunciation/relinquishment may not affect my military or selective service status, if any. I understand that any problems in this area must be resolved with the appropriate agencies.

8. My renunciation/relinquishment may not affect my liability, if any, to prosecution for any crimes which I may have committed or may commit in the future which violate United States law.

9. My renunciation/relinquishment may not affect my liability for extradition to the United States.

10. My renunciation/relinquishment may not exempt me from United States income taxation. With regard to United States taxation consequences, I understand that I must contact the United States Internal Revenue Service. Further, I understand that if my renunciation of United States citizenship is determined by the United States Attorney General to be motivated by tax avoidance purposes, I will be found excludable from the United States under Immigration and Nationality Act, as amended.

11. Upon renouncing/relinquishing my U.S. citizenship, I will no longer be able to transmit U.S. citizenship to my children born subsequent to this act.

12. The extremely serious and irrevocable nature of the act of renunciation/relinquishment has been explained to me by the *(Vice)* consul _____ Joel Fifield _____ at the American Embassy/Consulate General at _____ Asuncion, Paraguay _____ . I fully understand its consequences.

I: ☐ do   ☒ do not   choose to make a separate written explanation of my reasons for renouncing/relinquishing my United States citizenship.   I: ☒ swear   ☐ affirm   that I have.   ☒ read   ☐ had read to me this statement in the _____ English _____ language and fully understand its contents.

Name *(Typed)* _____ Glen Lee Roberts

Signature _____

DS-4081
05-2012

Page 1 of 2

48

CONSULAR OFFICER'S ATTESTATION

Glen Lee Roberts appeared personally and: [X] read [ ] had read to him/her this statement after my explanation of its meaning and the consequences of renunciation/relinquishment of United States citizenship and signed this statement: [ ] under oath [X] by affirmation before me this ___21___ day of

June , _2013_
(Month)   _(Year)_   _(Day)_

SEAL

Joel Fifield
Joel Fifield
Consul of the United States of America

DS-4081   Page 2 of 2

U.S. Department of State
BUREAU OF CONSULAR AFFAIRS

CERTIFICATE OF LOSS OF NATIONALITY OF THE UNITED STATES

This form is prescribed by the Secretary of State pursuant to Section 501 of the Act of
October 14, 1940 (54 Stat. 1171) and Section 358 of the Act of June 27, 1952 (66 Stat. 272).

DEPARTMENT USE ONLY

Embassy/Consulate _____Asuncion_____ of the United States of America

at _____Paraguay_____ ss:

I, _____Joel Fifield_____
Name

APPROVED
AMERICAN EMBASSY
ASUNCION
0 2 SET. 2014

DATE _____0 2 SET. 2014_____

hereby certify that, to the best of my knowledge and belief,

_____Glen Lee Roberts_____
Name

was born at _____Ann Arbor_____ _____Weshtenaw_____
Town or City   Province or County

_____Michigan_____ , on _____05-05-1962_____
State or Country   Date (mm-dd-yyyy)

That: he/she never resided in the United States (Dates*) _____

That: he/she resides at _____███████████████Asuncion, Paraguay_____

That: he/she acquired the nationality of the United States by virtue of birth in the U.S.A

That: he/she acquired the nationality of _____ by virtue of

That: he/she (The action causing expatriation should be set forth succinctly.) voluntary renunciation on Form DS-4080

That: said expatriating act was performed voluntarily with the intent to relinquish United States citizenship;

That: he/she thereby expatriated ___him___ self on (Date) _____06-21-2013_____ under the provisions of
(mm-dd-yyyy)

Section _____349 (a) (5)_____ of (The Nationality Act of 1940)* (The Immigration and Nationality Act of 1952 as amended)

That the evidence of such action consists of the following:
Forms DS-4079, DS-4080 and DS-4081

That attached to and made a part of this certificate are the following documents or copies thereof:
Copy of U.S. Passport # 426678401, issued on 07-02-2002

In testimony whereof, I have hereunto subscribed by name and affixed my office seal this ___21___ day of
_____June_____ , _____2013_____
(Month)   (Year)

[SEAL]

Signature

Joel Fifield
Title

*Strikeout inapplicable item.

DS-4083 (Formerly FS-348)
12-2007

SEE PAGE 2 FOR APPEAL PROCEDURES

Page 1 of 2

ADMINISTRATIVE REVIEW OF A FINDING OF LOSS OF NATIONALITY

The premise established by the administrative standard of evidence is applicable to cases adjudicated previously. Persons who previously lost U.S. citizenship may wish to have their cases reconsidered in light of this policy.

A person may initiate such a reconsideration by submitting a request to the nearest U.S. consular office or by writing directly to:

Director
Office of Policy Review and Inter-Agency Liaison
Overseas Citizens Services

(CA/OCS/PRI)
SA-29 4th Floor
Department of State
2201 C Street N.W.
Washington, D.C. 20520

or via express mail/courier service to:

Director
CA/OCS/PRI
2100 Pennsylvania Avenue N.W.
4th Floor
Washington, D.C. 20037

Each case will be reviewed on its own merits taking into consideration, for example, statements made by the person at the time of the potentially expatriating act.

For Additional Information See
http://www.travel.state.gov/law/citizenship/citizenship_778.html

DS-4083

7 FAM 1215 STATELESSNESS RESULTING FROM LOSS OF NATIONALITY

(CT:CON-262;   08-06-2008)

a. Persons who renounce their U.S. citizenship or commit any statutory act of expatriation intending thereby to relinquish such citizenship should understand that, unless they already possess a foreign nationality or are assured of acquiring another nationality shortly after completing their renunciation, they will become stateless and severe hardship to them could result. In the absence of a second nationality, those individuals would become stateless. Even if they possess permanent resident status in a foreign country, they could encounter difficulties continuing to reside there without a nationality.

b. The U.S. Government generally cannot accord stateless former U.S. nationals the consular assistance that is provided for U.S. citizens and U.S. noncitizen nationals pursuant to the Vienna Convention on Consular Relations (VCCR), U.S. statutes and regulations, and customary international law.

c. Stateless former U.S. nationals may also find it difficult or impossible to travel as they may not be issued a U.S. passport, and would probably not be able to obtain a passport or any other travel document from any country. Further, a person who has renounced U.S. citizenship will be required to apply for a visa to travel to the United States, just as other aliens do. If found ineligible for a visa, he or she could be permanently barred from the United States.

d. Expatriation will not necessarily prevent a former citizen's deportation from a foreign country to the United States, nor will it necessarily exempt that person from being prosecuted in the United States for any outstanding criminal charges or held liable for any military obligations or any taxes owed to the United States. The fact that a person has been rendered stateless does not serve to nullify the individual's expatriation if the renunciation is done voluntarily and with the intention to relinquish U.S. nationality.

e. In making all these points clear to potentially stateless renunciants, the Department of State will, nevertheless, afford them their right to expatriate. We will accept and approve renunciations of persons who do not already possess another nationality. It should be noted, however, that if a foreign state deports such individuals, he or she may find themselves deported to the United States, the country of their former nationality.

Renunciation and statelessness: Potential renunciants who do not possess another nationality or a claim to one are nonetheless permitted to renounce U.S. nationality. In doing so the individual becomes stateless. You should explain the extreme difficulties that a stateless individual may encounter trying to establish residency in a foreign country or traveling between countries in order to ensure that the individual understands the consequences of statelessness. See 7 FAM 1215 for additional information about statelessness. If the individual still desires to proceed with the renunciation, you may proceed.

9

U.S. State Department
Foreign Affairs Manual

7 FAM 1200
LOSS AND RESTORATION OF U.S. CITIZENSHIP

7 FAM 1210 INTRODUCTION

(CT:CON-445; 02-22-2013) (Office of Origin: CA/OCS/L)

7 FAM 1211 SUMMARY

(CT:CON-262; 08-06-2008)

Who may lose U.S. citizenship: A U.S. citizen by birth or naturalization INA 301 (8 U.S.C. 1401), INA 310 (8 U.S.C. 1421) or a U.S. noncitizen national INA 308 (8 U.S.C. 1408), INA 101(29) (8 U.S.C. 1101(29)) will lose U.S. nationality ("expatriate") her or himself by committing a statutory act of expatriation as defined in INA 349 (8 U.S.C. 1481), or predecessor statute, but only if the act is performed (1) voluntarily and (2) with the intention of relinquishing U.S. citizenship. The U.S. Supreme Court has spoken (Afroyim v. Rusk, 387 U.S. 253 (1967) and Vance v. Terrazas, 444 U.S. 252 (1980)): a person cannot lose U.S. nationality unless he or she voluntarily relinquishes that status. 7 FAM 1200 Appendix B provides a summary of U.S. Supreme Court decisions regarding loss of nationality.

Expatriation, like marriage and voting, is a personal elective right that cannot be exercised by another. Parents or legal guardians cannot renounce or relinquish the nationality of their children or wards, including adults who have been declared mentally incompetent. 7 FAM 1290 provides guidance regarding loss of nationality and minors, incompetents, prisoners, plea bargains, and other special circumstances.

Why expatriate: People elect to expatriate themselves for a variety of reasons: family reasons, tax reasons, pressure from foreign governments, and service as a diplomat from a foreign country, etc. Motivation is not relevant unless questions of duress and involuntariness arise. There is no requirement that persons disclose their motivation to a consular officer though it is often helpful if they do so in case they are acting based on a mistaken assumption.

Who has the burden of proving that loss of U.S. nationality occurred and what is the burden of proof: The party claiming that loss of citizenship occurred must establish this by a preponderance of the evidence. Black's Law Dictionary defines a preponderance of the evidence as "[g]reater weight of evidence, or evidence which is more credible and convincing to the mind." Preponderance of the evidence equates to "more likely than not." This is also known as the "balance of probabilities." This is the standard required in most civil cases.

The U.S. Supreme Court originally found that the criterion of persuasion was by evidence that was clear, unequivocal, and convincing, comparable to the burden of proof in denaturalization cases (Nishikawa v. Dulles, 356 U.S. 129, 78 S. Ct. 612, 2 L. Ed. 2d 659 (1958)); however, Congress explicitly modified this conclusion by legislation enacted in the Act of Sept. 26, 1961, § 19, 75 Stat. 656, applicable to actions or proceedings hereafter commenced, which specifies that a claim that loss of nationality occurred can be established by a preponderance of the evidence. (INA 349(b), 8 U.S.C. 1481(b)): The constitutionality of this statutory provision was upheld by the Supreme Court in the Vance v. Terrazas case, 444 U.S. 252 (1980).

NOTE ...

The standard of burden of proof for loss of nationality, preponderance of the evidence, differs from the much higher standards of ...

Beyond a reasonable doubt - this is the standard required by the prosecution in most criminal cases within an adversarial system. This means that the proposition being presented by the government must be proven to the extent that there is no "reasonable doubt" in the mind of a reasonable person that the defendant is guilty. There can still be a doubt, but only to the extent that it would not affect a "reasonable person's" belief that the defendant is guilty. If the doubt that is raised does affect a "reasonable person's" belief that the defendant is guilty, the jury is not satisfied beyond a "reasonable doubt"; or

Clear and convincing evidence – This is an intermediate level of burden of persuasion sometimes employed in the U.S. civil procedure. In order to prove something by "clear and convincing evidence" the party with the burden of proof must convince the trier of fact that it is substantially more likely than not that the thing is in fact true. This is a lesser requirement than "proof beyond a reasonable doubt" which requires that the trier of fact be close to certain of the truth of the matter asserted, but a stricter requirement than proof by "preponderance of the evidence," which merely requires that the matter asserted seem more likely true than not.

Four elements must be established before a finding of loss may be made:

The person is in fact a U.S. citizen;

The person committed an act that is potentially expatriating under INA 349(a) (8 U.S.C. 1481(a));

The person committed the act voluntarily. A person who commits a potentially expatriating act is presumed to have done so voluntarily, but the presumption may be rebutted upon a showing, by a preponderance of the evidence, that the act or acts committed or performed were not done voluntarily. (INA 349(b), 8 U.S.C. 1481(b)); and

The person intended to relinquish the rights and privileges of U.S. citizenship. If the would-be renunciant/person relinquishing U.S. citizenship demonstrates a clear intention to resume his/her residency in the United States without applying for a U.S. visa, the intention to relinquish U.S. citizenship has not been established satisfactorily and a finding of non-loss should be made.

Where must the expatriating act occur: The expatriating act, except for an oath of renunciation taken during the course of a state of war or conviction of treason and certain other crimes, must be committed overseas for it to be effective; however, a potentially expatriating act performed in the United States may thereafter result in the loss of citizenship if the citizen thereafter takes up residence in a foreign country. (INA 351, 8 U.S.C. 1483(a)). INA 349(a)(6) provides for renunciation of U.S. citizenship in the United States before such officer as may be designated by the Attorney General, whenever the United States shall be in a state of war and the Attorney General shall approve such renunciation as not contrary to the interests of national defense. The U.S. Departments of Justice and Homeland Security have not promulgated regulations implementing this provision. There is no requirement that a U.S. citizen renouncing or relinquishing U.S. citizenship abroad be a resident of the U.S. consular district.

Relinquish v. renounce: INA 349(a)(5) prescribes how renunciation of U.S. citizenship must occur. This is explained in detail in 7 FAM 1280. A citizen may also voluntarily relinquish U.S. citizenship upon committing voluntarily one of the other potentially expatriating acts enumerated in INA 349 and possessing the requisite intent to relinquish. The distinction becomes meaningful when a person who has been found to have lost U.S. citizenship later requests an appeal or administrative review of that decision. It is much more difficult to establish a lack of intent or duress for renunciation of U.S. citizenship.

No temporary suspension of U.S. citizenship: A person cannot renounce or relinquish U.S. citizenship temporarily or put his or her U.S. citizenship "in suspense" while, for example, accepting a diplomatic appointment from a foreign government. A loss of citizenship is permanent and irrevocable, unless the U.S. Government subsequently overturns the loss for involuntariness or lack of intent. Individuals who lose citizenship would need to reacquire it though naturalization.

No retroactive effect on derivative citizenship: Unlike denaturalization, loss of nationality operates only for the future, and has no retroactive effect. The expatriated citizen's status was lawfully acquired, and its termination does not affect previous events. For this reason, a person's loss of nationality does not affect citizenship or immigration status previously acquired on the basis of the principal's citizenship, unless the effective date of loss of U.S. citizenship pre-dated the time when a benefit accrued based on the fact that the person was believed to be a U.S. citizen. Thus, the loss of nationality does not terminate the citizenship of the principal's children, acquired derivatively through their parent prior to the parent's loss of nationality. For this reason, it often has been necessary to determine the precise date of expatriation, since children born abroad before that date may have acquired U.S. citizenship, while those born after that date would have no such claim.

7 FAM 1212 FORMS TO BE USED IN DEVELOPING A LOSS-OF-NATIONALITY CASE

(CT:CON-437; 01-29-2013)

The following Department of State forms have been approved to develop and document a loss-of-nationality case:

Form DS-4079, Questionnaire - Information for Determining Possible Loss of U.S. Citizenship;

Form DS-4083, Certificate of Loss of Nationality of the United States ("CLN");

Form DS-4080, Oath of Renunciation of the Nationality of the United States;

Form DS-4081, Statement of Understanding Concerning the Consequences and Ramifications of Relinquishment or Renunciation of U.S. Citizenship; and

Form DS-4082, Witnesses' Attestation Renunciation/Relinquishment of Citizenship: To be used only when the person relinquishing or renouncing citizenship does not speak English.

Effective the publication date of this subchapter, the Bureau of Consular Affairs (CA) is reinstating the use of the new questionnaire, Form DS-4079 in developing a loss-of-nationality case if the citizen states there was an intent to relinquish U.S. citizenship when performing the potentially expatriating act:

The Department (CA/OCS and L/CA) have determined that the new questionnaire Form DS-4079 is an important element in developing a loss-of-nationality case;

In 1995, CA discontinued use of the questionnaire in loss-of-nationality cases under INA 349(a)(1); INA 349(a)(2), INA 349(a)(3) and INA 349(a)(4) (1995 State 034894);

A questionnaire was used between March 30, 1984, and February 10, 1995;

For guidance about documentation required by the Department for loss-of-nationality cases prior to 1984, consult CA/OCS/L at ASK-OCS-L@state.gov.

7 FAM 1213 RESPONSIBILITY FOR LOSS-OF-NATIONALITY CASES

(CT:CON-445; 02-22-2013)

Who may prepare a Certificate of Loss of Nationality (CLN) and accompanying documents:

INA 358 authorizes a diplomatic or consular officer to certify facts on which it is believed a U.S. citizen may have lost citizenship. (Note that the consular officer's finding is not self-executing. Actual approval of the finding of loss of nationality can only be made by the Department, Form DS-4083, formerly; Form FS-348, is used to record and certify loss of citizenship. INA 358 applies to cases arising under Chapter IV NA (Section 401 to 410 inclusive), and to Chapter 3, Title III INA 349 to INA 357 inclusive. Cases involving loss under the Act of 1907 are rare; when these cases arise, the consular officer should seek advice from CA/OCS/L (*ASK-OCS-L@state.gov*);

A CLN is not prepared when citizenship was lost through failure to comply with the retention provisions of former INA 301(b), prior to its repeal, effective October 10, 1978 (see 7 FAM 1131.7 and 7 FAM 1100 Appendix L.;

A consular officer at a U.S. embassy or consulate abroad may prepare a preliminary recommendation of a finding of loss of nationality in the form prescribed and transmit it to the Office of American Citizen Services and Crisis Management (CA/OCS/ACS) for approval.

Who may approve a Certificate of Loss of Nationality: The authority to approve or disapprove a finding of loss of nationality is a grave responsibility; consequently, the Department of State has imposed a high level of checks and balances for such decision making. This is the one area of citizenship and nationality law which has not been and absent a change in the statute cannot be delegated to U.S. consular officers abroad:

> Only a division chief in the Office of American Citizen Services and Crisis Management (CA/OCS/ACS) in the Directorate of Overseas Citizens Services, Bureau of Consular Affairs of the Department of State, may approve a Certificate of Loss of Nationality;

> If the CA/OCS/ACS Division Chief is not available, the Acting Division Chief may approve a Certificate of Loss of Nationality, only if a formal delegation of authority memo from the Division Chief to the Acting Division Chief, cleared by the Director of CA/OCS/ACS exists;

> CA/OCS/ACS should consult CA/OCS/L for guidance before making a finding of loss of nationality in the following circumstances:

> Any case involving mental impairment;

> Any case involving a prisoner/plea bargain;

> Any case involving a minor or a person near the age of 18;

> Any case of a person taking up a high-level position in a foreign government;

> Any case of a person serving in the armed forces of a foreign state engaged in hostilities against the United States;

> Any case involving a person who is a member of a cult or other community in which persons are relinquishing or renouncing U.S. citizenship as a group; or

> Any case in which a person makes statements, in the citizenship questionnaire or a supplementary statement, which are contradictory or ambiguous with respect to his or her intent to relinquish U.S. citizenship or the voluntariness of his/her actions.

Who may conduct an administrative review of a previous finding of loss of nationality:

> The office making the original determination of loss of nationality should not conduct the administrative review;

> All reconsideration of previous findings of loss of nationality must be conducted by CA/OCS/L.

An attorney cannot be assigned the reconsideration if he or she was consulted by CA/OCS/ACS regarding the original finding of loss of nationality;

As appropriate, CA/OCS/L will confer with the Office of the Assistant Legal Adviser for Consular Affairs (L/CA). CA/OCS/L will confer with L/CA in each case in which CA/OCS/L proposes to sustain a CLN;

The role of CA/OCS/L in administrative review of loss of nationality and in vacating a CLN replaces the formal appeal procedure previously provided by the Board of Appellate Review (L/BAR). 22 CFR 7.2 provides that "the Department may administratively vacate a CLN on its own initiative at any time."

7 FAM 1214 AUTHORITY

(CT:CON-439; 02-05-2013)

The Secretary of State has statutory authority to determine whether a person not in the United States is a U.S. citizen or noncitizen national, including whether a person who was a U.S. citizen or noncitizen national has lost U.S. nationality. INA 104(a)(3) (8 U.S.C. 1104(a)(3)) and INA 358(8 U.S.C. 1501). The Department of State also makes nationality determinations, including loss-of-nationality determinations, when adjudicating passport applications, because only a U.S. citizen or U.S. noncitizen national may be issued a U.S. passport.

Immigration and Nationality Act of 1952, as amended:

The grounds for loss of nationality enumerated in the Nationality Act of 1940 were codified and again expanded in the Immigration and Nationality Act of 1952 (Public Law No. 82-414, §§ 349-357, 66 Statutes at Large 267). The law which applies, e.g., the Nationality Act of 1940 or the INA, is the law in effect on the date of the potentially expatriating act;

Early amendments of the statute tended to enhance its severity;

Act of Sept. 3, 1954, § 2, 68 Statutes at Large 1146 (adding as grounds for loss of citizenship conviction for certain crimes, including rebellion and insurrection, seditious conspiracy, and advocating forceful overthrow of the U.S. Government); Act of Sept. 26, 1961, § 19, 75 Statutes at Large 656 (adding *INA 401(c)*, 8 U.S.C. 1481(c));

However, as a result of later Supreme Court decisions, Congress adopted amendments in 1986 which simplified and liberalized the statute, and emphasized the need for an intention to lose nationality (Immigration and Nationality Act Amendments of 1986, Public Law No. 99-653, § 18, 100 Statutes at Large 3655). Section 18(a) of Public Law 99-653 provided that Subsection (a) of INA 349 (8 U.S.C. 1481) was amended by inserting "voluntarily performing any of the following acts with the intention of relinquishing United States nationality:" after "shall lose his nationality by";

An amendment of the statute in 1986 eliminated the provision allowing for approval of the foreign military service by the Secretaries of State and Defense and provided that a U.S. national who has attained the age of 18 would potentially lose U.S. nationality by entering or serving in the armed forces of a foreign state if such armed forces were engaged in hostilities against the United States or if the person served as a commissioned or noncommissioned officer of such foreign armed forces. Immigration and Nationality Act Amendments of 1986, Public Law No. 99-653, § 18(d), 100 Stat. 3658 (amending INA 349(a)(3), 8 U.S.C. 1481(a)(3));

Public Law 103-416, the Immigration and Nationality Technical Corrections Act of 1994, 108 Statutes at Large 4305, amended INA 358 of the Immigration and Nationality Act (8 U.S.C. 1501) by adding at the end the following new sentence: "Approval by the Secretary of State of a certificate under this section shall constitute a final administrative determination of loss of United States nationality under this Act, subject to such procedures for administrative appeal as the Secretary may prescribe by regulation, and also shall constitute a denial of a right or privilege of United States nationality for purposes of section 360";

Chart: INA 349 and developments in subsequent rulings by the U.S. Supreme Court and statutory amendments:

ExpatriatingAct	Section of Law	Notes
Naturalization in a foreign state	8 U.S.C. 1481(a)(1) INA 349(a)(1)	After attaining age 18
Taking oath of allegiance to a foreign state	8 U.S.C. 1481(a)(2) INA	After attaining age 18

	349(a)(2)	
Service in the armed forces of a foreign state	8 U.S.C. 1481(a)(3) INA 349(a)(3)	(A) If such armed forces are engaged in hostilities against the United States; or (B) If such persons serve as a commissioned or noncommissioned officer.
Employment by a foreign state	8 U.S.C. 1481(a)(4) INA 349(a)(4)	If after attaining age 18 … (A) He or she has or acquires the nationality of such foreign state; or (B) For such position an oath, affirmation or declaration of allegiance is required
Renunciation of U.S. citizenship abroad	8 U.S.C. 1481(a)(5) INA 349(a)(5)	NOTE: Formerly numbered 8 U.S.C. 1481(a)(6); see Afroyim v. Rusk, 387 U.S. 253 (1967) (eliminating voting in a foreign election as an expatriating act)
Renunciation of U.S. citizenship while in the United States	8 U.S.C. 1481(a)(6) INA 349(a)(6)	1. Before officer designated by the Attorney General; 2. Whenever the United States shall be in a state of war; and 3. The Attorney General shall approve such renunciation not contrary to the interests of national defense NOTE: The Attorney General and Secretary of DHS have not
		designated an officer to receive domestic

		renunciations; Formerly numbered INA 349(a)(7) renumbered when Afroyim decision eliminated INA 349(a)(5) Voting in a Political Election	
Treason against the United States	8 U.S.C. 1481(a)(7) INA 349(a)(7)	Formerly numbered INA 349(a)(9) renumbered when 8 U.S.C. 1481(a)(8) Deserting the Armed Forces of the United States at Time of War declared unconstitutional	
Former grounds for loss, declared unconstitutional: Voting in a foreign	INA 349(a)(5) as originally	Declared unconstitutional: Afroyim v. Rusk; see 7 FAM 1200 Appendix B _____ _____	

| election | enacted; 8 U.S.C. 1481(a)(5) | Declared unconstitutional: Trop v. Dulles, 356 U.S. 86, 78 S. Ct. 590, 2 L. Ed. 2d 630 (1958); repealed in 1978 as amended by Immigration and Nationality Act Amendments of 1986, Public Law No. 99-653, § 18(a), 100 Stat. 3658. | |
| Deserting the armed forces of the United States at time of war, if and when convicted thereof by court martial and dishonorably discharged | | | |

Departing from or	INA	Declared unconstitutional:	
remaining outside of	349(a)(10	Kennedy v. Mendoza-Martinez, 372	
the United States in	); 8	U.S. 144, 83 S. Ct. 554, 92 L. Ed.	
time of war or period	U.S.C.	644 (1963)	
declared by the	1481(a)(1	Notes:	
President to be a period	0)	1. An 1865 statute	
of national emergency		providing for loss of citizenship by draft evaders	
for the		was repealed in 1940	
purpose of evading or avoiding		2. Legislation, enacted in 1944 and	
training and service in		codified in the Act of 1952,	
the armed forces of the		prescribed loss of nationality for	
United States.		departing from or remaining outside the United States during time of war or declared national emergency in	

		order to evade or avoid service in the armed forces of the United States	
		3. These statutory provisions were	

		declared unconstitutional by the Supreme Court (Kennedy v. Mendoza-Martinez, 372 U.S. 144, 83 S. Ct. 554, 92 Lawyers Edition (L. Ed.) 644 (1963) and were repealed by Congress in 1976, Footnote 297, National Emergencies Act of 1976, Public Law No. 94-412, § 501(a), 90 Statutes at Large. 1255, 1258; see Senate Report No. 1168, 94th Congress., 2d Session. 32 (1976), reprinted in 1976 U.S.C.C.A.N. 2288; House of Representatives Report No. 238, 94th Congress., 2d Session 15 (1975).
Seeking and claiming a benefit of a foreign nationality acquired at	INA 350 (8 U.S.C. 1482)	Repealed prospectively October 10, 1978 Public Law 95-432 See 7 FAM 1200 Appendix D

birth by a person born a citizen of the United States		
Naturalized citizen taking up residence in former country of origin	INA 352 (8 U.S.C. 1484)	Declared Unconstitutional: Schneider v. Rusk, 377 U.S. 163 (1964); repealed Public Law 95-432 on October 10, 1978; see 7 FAM 1200 Appendix D

The Nationality Act of 1940 (54 Statutes at Large 1137) considerably enlarged the grounds for loss of nationality:

In addition to naturalization in or oath of allegiance to a foreign state, the enumerated acts of expatriation were extended to include military or government service for a foreign government, voting in a foreign political election, formal renunciation of citizenship, deserting the armed forces in time of war, treason, and specified residence in foreign countries by naturalized citizens;

Chart: Nationality Act of 1940 and developments in subsequent rulings by the U.S. Supreme Court and statutory amendments:

Expatriating Act	Section of Law	Notes
Naturalization in a foreign state	Section 401(a) NA	

Taking an oath or affirmation of allegiance to a foreign state	Section 401(b) NA	After attaining age 18
Entering, serving in the armed forces of a foreign state	Section 401(c) NA	
Accepting position in a foreign government for which only nationals are eligible	Section 401(d) NA	
Voting in foreign election	Section 401(e) NA	Declared unconstitutional: Afroyim v. Rusk; see 8 FAM 1200 Appendix B
Renunciation of U.S. citizenship	Section 401(f) NA	
Deserting the United States Military or Naval Service in time of war	Section 401(g) NA	Declared unconstitutional: Trop v. Dulles; see 7 FAM 1200 Appendix B
Treason	Section 401(h) NA	

The Expatriation Act of 1907 (Act of March 2, 1907, 34 Statutes at Large 1228) largely codified prior executive interpretations, specified that loss of citizenship would occur by naturalization in or oath of allegiance to a foreign state, that a U.S. citizen woman who married a foreigner would take the nationality of her husband, and that when a naturalized citizen lived in a foreign state for certain periods it was presumed that he or she ceased to be a U.S. citizen. In spelling out the grounds for loss of nationality the 1907 Act made provision for effectuating the citizen's apparent wishes. In addition, it introduced a new concept by prescribing situations in which citizenship could be lost without regard to such desires.

Related statutes:

26 U.S.C. 6039G Information on Individuals Losing U.S. Citizenship (Internal Revenue Code);

18 U.S.C. 922G Unlawful Acts – Sale of Firearms to Renunciants (Brady Act).

Regulatory authority: (Current 22 CFR 50.40 Certificate of Loss of U.S. Nationality; 22 CFR 50.50 Renunciation of Nationality; 22 CFR 50.51 Notice of Right to Appeal). CA/OCS/L is in the process of revising 22 CFR Part 50, including to eliminate the Board of Appellate Review.

7 FAM 1215 STATELESSNESS RESULTING FROM LOSS OF NATIONALITY

(CT:CON-262; 08-06-2008)

Persons who renounce their U.S. citizenship or commit any statutory act of expatriation intending thereby to relinquish such citizenship should understand that, unless they already possess a foreign nationality or are assured of acquiring another nationality shortly after completing their renunciation, they will become stateless and severe hardship to them could result. In the absence of a second nationality, those individuals would become stateless. Even if they possess permanent resident status in a foreign country, they could encounter difficulties continuing to reside there without a nationality.

The U.S. Government generally cannot accord stateless former U.S. nationals the consular assistance that is provided for U.S. citizens and U.S. noncitizen nationals pursuant to the Vienna Convention on Consular Relations (VCCR), U.S. statutes and regulations, and customary international law.

Stateless former U.S. nationals may also find it difficult or impossible to travel as they may not be issued a U.S. passport, and would probably not be able to obtain a passport or any other travel document from any country. Further, a person who has renounced U.S. citizenship will be required to apply for a visa to travel to the United States, just as other aliens do. If found ineligible for a visa, he or she could be permanently barred from the United States.

Expatriation will not necessarily prevent a former citizen's deportation from a foreign country to the United States, nor will it necessarily exempt that person from being prosecuted in the United States for any outstanding criminal charges or held liable for any military obligations or any taxes owed to the United States. The fact that a person has been rendered stateless does not serve to nullify the individual's expatriation if the renunciation is done voluntarily and with the intention to relinquish U.S. nationality.

In making all these points clear to potentially stateless renunciants, the Department of State will, nevertheless, afford them their right to expatriate. We will accept and approve renunciations of persons who do not already possess another nationality. It should be noted, however, that if a foreign state deports such individuals, he or she may find themselves deported to the United States, the country of their former nationality.

7 FAM 1216 VISA REQUIREMENTS FOR FORMER U.S. CITIZENS AND VISA EXCLUDABILITY

(CT:CON-262; 08-06-2008)

a. Visa requirements for former U.S. citizens: An expatriate is subject to all of the requirements for entry to the United States that apply to other aliens, including visa requirements, and to all of the grounds of visa denial and inadmissibility for aliens.

Visa excludability for persons found by the Attorney General to have renounced U.S. citizenship for the purposes of avoiding taxation: The Illegal Immigration Reform and Immigrant Responsibility Act of 1996 (IIRAIRA) (Public Law 104-208) added 212(a)(10)(E) to the Immigration and Nationality Act (8 U.S.C.

1182 (a)(10)(E)). INA 212(a)(10)(E) made inadmissible "any alien who is a former citizen of the United States who officially renounces United States citizenship and who is determined by the Attorney General to have renounced United States citizenship for the purpose of avoiding taxation." This amendment applies only to individuals who renounced U.S. citizenship on or after the effective date of the Act, September 30, 1996. (See 9 FAM 40.105 N1 Applicability of INA 212(a)(10)(E).) The Attorney General's authority transferred to the Secretary of Homeland Security under the Homeland Security Act of 2002. The Department of Homeland Security has not published implementing regulations on INA 212(a)(10)(E) (8 U.S.C. 1182), so no procedures implementing this law are currently in effect.

7 FAM 1217 THROUGH 1219 UNASSIGNED

7 FAM 1220 UNAVAILABLE

7 FAM 1230

ADMINISTRATIVE REVIEW AND APPEAL OF LOSS-OF-NATIONALITY FINDINGS

(CT:CON-469; 07-31-2013) (Office of Origin: CA/OCS/L)

7 FAM 1231 INTRODUCTION

(CT:CON-289; 03-26-2009)

> Persons held to have lost (or not lost) U.S. nationality by performance of acts made expatriating by statute have the right to request an administrative review of the finding as part of the due process of law guaranteed by the Fourteenth Amendment of the U.S. Constitution. INA 349(b) (8 U.S.C. 1481(b)) places the burden of proof "upon the party claiming that loss has occurred."

> On October 20, 2008, the Department of State published a Final Rule, Public Notice 6398 in Federal Register, Vol. 73, No. 203, pages 62196-62197 eliminating the Department's Board of Appellate Review in the Office of the

Legal Adviser (L/BAR). The Rule revised 22 CFR 7 and 22 CFR 50 and authorized on a discretionary basis an alternative less cumbersome review of loss of nationality determinations by the Bureau of Consular Affairs (CA). The Interim Final Rule published at 74 FR 41256 July 18, 2008 was adopted without change.

The procedures for requesting an administrative review or appeal of the Department's administrative holding of loss of nationality are shown on the reverse side of Form DS-4083, Certificate of Loss of Nationality of the United States.

The availability of an administrative review without time limitation does not constitute a mandatory procedure for administrative appeal. The passage of time does not preclude a review particularly since loss of U.S. nationality is an area of the law which has undergone substantial change and older cases are sometimes those most deserving of review.

7 FAM 1232 AUTHORITY TO CONDUCT ADMINISTRATIVE REVIEW OF LOSS DECISIONS

(CT:CON-469; 07-31-2013)

Upon revision of the regulations, the Bureau of Consular Affairs, Directorate of Overseas Citizens Services, Office of Legal Affairs (CA/OCS/L) is solely responsible for the administrative review of previous findings of loss (or nonloss) of U.S. citizenship.

7 FAM 1234 provides guidance about procedures to be followed by CA/OCS/L in recording actions taken in loss-of-nationality cases in the American Citizen Services (ACS) System and the Passport Lookout and Support System (PLOTS).

Inquirers should be advised to direct a written request for an administrative review to the following address and to include information regarding their intention to relinquish U.S. citizenship at the time of the commission of the expatriating act and the voluntariness of the expatriating act:

Express Mail:

Director

Office of Legal Affairs (CA/OCS/L)
Overseas Citizens Services
Bureau of Consular Affairs
U.S. Department of State
600 19th Street N.W.
10th Floor

Washington, DC 20431
Email: Ask-OCS-L@state.gov

Regular Mail:

Director
U.S. Department of State
CA/OCS/L
SA-17, 10th Floor
Washington, DC 20522-1710

7 FAM 1233 FINDINGS OF LOSS OF NATIONALITY DECLARED UNCONSTITUTIONAL BY THE U.S. SUPREME COURT

(CT:CON-449; 03-25-2013)

If the statute under which the finding of loss of nationality was made has been declared unconstitutional by the U.S. Supreme Court, no formal administrative review of the case by CA/OCS/L is necessary.

If a Consular Lookout and Support System (CLASS) CLASS reason code Q (questionable claim to U.S. citizenship) or CLASS reason code L (loss of nationality) occurs for one of the following reasons:

Expatriating Act	Section of Law	Notes	
Deserting the armed forces of the	INA 349(a)(8)	Declared	
United States at time of war, if	8 U.S.C.	unconstitutio nal:	
and when convicted thereof by	1481(a)(8)	Trop v. Dulles	
court martial and dishonorably		(1958)	
discharged.	Section 401(g)	See 7 FAM 1200	
	Nationality	Appendix B	

	Act of 1940		
	(NA)		
Departing from or remaining outside	INA 349(a)(10)	Declared	
of the United States in time of war	8 U.S.C.	unconstitutio nal:	
or period declared by the	1481(a)(10)	Kennedy v.	
President to be a period of		Mendoza-Martinez	
national emergency for the		(1963)	
purpose of evading or avoiding		See 7 FAM 1200	
training and service in the armed		Appendix B	
forces of the United States.			
Naturalized citizen taking up	INA 352	Declared	
residence in former country of	8 U.S.C. 1484	unconstitutio nal:	
origin		Schneider v. Rusk	
		(1964)	
		See 7 FAM 1200	
		Appendix B	
Voting in a	INA 349(a)(5)	Declared	

foreign election			
	as originally	unconstitutio nal:	
	enacted	Afroyim v. Rusk	
	Section 401(e)	(1967)	
	NA	See 7 FAM 1200	
		Appendix B	

Domestic passport agencies/centers: The authorized passport specialist should delete the lookout and issue the passport.

Posts abroad: Consular officers abroad are not authorized to remove CLASS entries; consequently, they should contact CA/OCS/L (Ask-OCS-L@state.gov) to have the lookout removed.

If a Certificate of Loss of Nationality (CLN) was approved for the case, CA/OCS/L (Ask-OCS-L@state.gov) should be asked to retrieve the manual record and vacate the CLN. The PLOTS record should be updated accordingly.

If the "Q" lookout was entered in CLASS prior to 1990, when the administrative presumption that a U.S. citizen intends to retain U.S. nationality when he or she commits certain acts was adopted (see 7 FAM 1222), CA/OCS/ACS can review the case and remove the lookout as appropriate. This authorization relates to:

INA 349(a)(1) naturalization in a foreign state;

INA 349(a)(2) taking an oath of allegiance to a foreign state; and

INA 349(a)(4) serving in a low-level position in the government of a foreign state.

CA/OCS/L presumes that one who has served in the military of a state not engaged in hostilities with the United States intends to retain one's U.S. citizenship.

7 FAM 1234 RECORD KEEPING IN ADMINSTRATIVE REVIEW OF LOSS-OF-NATIONALITY CASES

(CT:CON-407; 06-29-2012)

It is important that meticulous records be maintained of actions taken by the Department (CA and posts abroad) in loss-of-nationality cases.

When a request for an administrative review of a previous finding of loss of nationality is received in CA/OCS/L, the previous case record will be retrieved from PLOTS and the Passport Issuance Electronic Records System (PIERS).

The CA/OCS/L attorney should complete the administrative review and prepare an advisory opinion on the case within 30 days of receipt, or provide written notice to the post, requester or requester's attorney that additional time will be required:

The CA/OCS/L attorney should prepare an interim response acknowledging receipt of the request for administrative review;

The office director should concur with the advisory opinion and the notification letter to the requester prepared by the attorney adviser. If necessary and appropriate, the Office of the Legal Adviser for Consular Affairs (L/CA) should be consulted;

The CA/OCS/L attorney or office director will provide the ACS Office Director with a copy of the administrative review and advisory opinion, for appropriate feedback and follow-up within CA/OCS/ACS to ensure uniformity of ACS loss of nationality decision making;

If the finding of loss of nationality is reversed, the attorney adviser should ensure that the lookout is removed from CLASS via PLOTS; and

The correspondence should also be added to the PLOTS record to ensure that passport agencies and centers have access to the information. Not all Department offices have access to the ACS system.

7 FAM 1235 FACTORS TO BE CONSIDERED IN CONDUCTING ADMINISTRATIVE REVIEW OF PREVIOUS FINDINGS OF LOSS OF NATIONALITY

(CT:CON-407; 06-29-2012)

Some cases in which the Department had previously held loss of nationality may be reversed administratively by the Department. Advantages of this procedure are that it is less expensive to the person appealing and more convenient. This is not a substitute for the person's right to appeal the decision in a court of law but is an option available in some cases.

This procedure may be followed when:

The law under which the holding of loss of nationality was made is later held unconstitutional; for example, a law concerning voting in a foreign election;

A major change in the interpretation of the law on expatriation is made as a result of a U.S. Supreme Court decision; for example, the decision in Afroyim v. Rusk or Vance v. Terrazas;

A major change is made in the interpretation of the law by the Department or is made by another agency and adopted by the Department. Most of these changes arose under previous statutes and prior to the decision in Afroyim v. Rusk; for example, cases involving naturalization of a minor; and

Substantial new evidence of involuntariness or intent, not previously considered but contemporaneous to the time when the potentially expatriating act was performed, is presented by the individual.

CA/OCS/L will review a finding of loss of citizenship at any time at the request of the individual concerning whom the CLN has been approved, under the doctrine that an administrative agency has the ability to review its earlier decisions. In conducting an administrative review of a previous finding of loss of citizenship, CA/OCS/L examines whether the individual who expatriated herself or himself did so voluntarily with the intention of relinquishing U.S. citizenship and whether the appropriate procedures were followed in the particular case under review.

7 FAM 1236 REVIEWING THE RECORD

(CT:CON-407; 06-29-2012)

The first action CA/OCS/L will take is to retrieve the loss-of-nationality file, lookout and previous passport history of the applicant.

CA/OCS/L will consider whether the preponderance of the evidence shows that it is more likely than not that the individual intended to lose U.S. nationality.

CA/OCS/L will consider whether the individual has overcome the voluntariness presumption and demonstrated that it is more likely than not that the act was involuntary.

The individual's signing of an Affidavit of Expatriated Person or Statement of

Voluntary Relinquishment does not preclude the vacating of a previously approved CLN; however, in such an instance, it is incumbent upon the individual to present evidence of factors such as parental coercion, mental infirmity, misinformation provided by a consular officer, etc., that would refute the contents of the affidavit. All such evidence must relate to the time when the potentially expatriating act was performed and not to a subsequent "change of heart."

Particular care should be given to reviewing "older" findings of loss of U.S. citizenship; i.e., those occurring prior to 1970 and, to a lesser degree, to cases decided in the period between 1970-1990. Bear in mind that during this period, the law of expatriation underwent radical changes as a result of a number of U.S. Supreme Court decisions. The net effect of these changes was to require that the Department find that the preponderance of the evidence establishes that an individual intended to lose nationality before approving a CLN. Please note that there was a significant lag during this period between (1) U.S. Supreme Court decisions on expatriation and (2) their full implementation by the Department, and some U.S. consular officers may not have understood that they could not simply presume a person's intent to relinquish U.S. citizenship. Also be aware that, particularly before 1980, a person who had performed a potentially expatriating act usually was denied a U.S. passport while contesting a finding of loss of U.S. citizenship, and was not considered eligible to receive a visa to travel to the United States because that he or she had not yet been determined to be an alien. In cases when persons had an urgent need to travel to the United States (e.g., serious illness of a close family member) many have credibly recounted that they resolved this dilemma by relinquishing U.S. citizenship so that they could receive visas and make the trip.

Contemporaneous evidence of intent: As noted in this section, the relevant intent is the person's intent at the time of the commission of the potentially expatriating act. Thus, evidence submitted generally should relate back to the time of the potentially expatriating act, i.e., the person's frame of mind at that time or circumstances which are illuminating with respect to the person's intent toward U.S. citizenship at that time. Persons providing affidavits, for example, generally should have first-hand knowledge of events at the time when the statutory act was performed rather than information based upon another's recounting of them. Note, however, that a person's behavior before or after the expatriating act can be relevant to the determination of the intent at the time of the act.

Voluntariness and renunciation: Renunciation cases generally will involve the issue of voluntariness rather than intent. This is because a person renouncing U.S. nationality expressly attests to an intention to lose U.S. nationality by signing the Statement of Understanding and Oath of Renunciation (see 7 FAM 1280). However, if the intent was misinformed (based upon an error(s) of law or fact related by the consular officer to the renunciant at that time), it may be determined that the intent was not knowing and that therefore the intent required by law was not present.

Mental illness or incompetence: Cases involving persons with a history of mental illness or developmental mental incompetence who have chosen to renounce U.S. citizenship, require careful review. It is not required that there be a showing of mental incompetence but rather that some impairment of judgment occurred such as to refute, by a preponderance of the evidence, the presumption of voluntariness which would otherwise apply (see 7 FAM 1290).

Renunciation under the age of 18 or shortly after attaining age 18: Similarly, careful attention should be given to persons who renounced U.S. citizenship in the time period before, or shortly after, their 18th birthday. In many instances, and in many societies, it is not unusual for such persons to be especially vulnerable to parental pressure despite contemporary denials of any such pressure. While persons may be legally emancipated, they may well be particularly subject to the undue influence of another, e.g., a parent (see 7 FAM 1290). In such instances, it may be useful to obtain affidavits from the renunciant's parents indicating the absence of parental pressure.

7 FAM 1237 INTERVIEWING THE PERSON SEEKING RECONSIDERATION

(CT:CON-407; 06-29-2012)

CA/OCS/L may ask a consular officer to interview or convene a video teleconference with the individual residing abroad to obtain information regarding the voluntariness of the latter's actions in relinquishing her or his citizenship and/or her or his intentions with respect to the retention of U.S. citizenship at the time of the commission of the expatriating act.

7 FAM 1238 REVERSING FINDING OF LOSS OF NATIONALITY, VACATING CLN AND REMOVING CLASS LOOKOUT

(CT:CON-407; 06-29-2012)

If CA/OCS/L decides to reverse the finding of loss of nationality and vacate the CLN, the individual's U.S. nationality is restored as of the date of the commission of the expatriating act that had served initially as the basis for the approval of the CLN.

CA/OCS/L will communicate the decision to the individual and the post.

CA/OCS/L will affix a specific stamp to the CLN reflecting that the CLN is vacated. The stamp notes the date of the decision, how the post and subject were notified of the decision, and bears the signature of the CA/OCS/L official making this determination.

CA/OCS/L will remove the name from CLASS, close the PLOTS record, and update the ACS record. Copies of correspondence will be incorporated in the ACS and PLOTS records.

CA/OCS/L will officially inform relevant federal agencies that the finding of loss has been overturned (see 7 FAM 1240).

7 FAM 1239 LACK OF SUPPORT TO REVERSE PREVIOUS FINDING OF LOSS

(CT:CON-407; 06-29-2012)

If CA/OCS/L determines that there is inadequate support in the application and the record to reverse the CLN and that the finding of loss should in all likelihood be sustained, CA/OCS/L, after consultation with L/CA in appropriate cases, will notify the individual and/or his/her representative, and the post as needed, advising that additional evidence to support vacating the CLN should be provided and that failure to submit additional evidence within a prescribed time period will result in the filing of the application for overturning the loss of nationality.

7 FAM 1240

INTERAGENCY COORDINATION AND REPORTING REQUIREMENTS

(CT:CON-449; 03-25-2013) (Office of Origin: CA/OCS/L)

7 FAM 1241 INTRODUCTION TO INTERAGENCY COORDINATION AND REPORTING REQUIREMENTS

(CT:CON-407; 06-29-2012)

The Bureau of Consular Affairs (CA) coordinates closely with various offices in the Department of State and other Federal agencies, and with U.S. States, on issues related to expatriation. Much of this interagency coordination is mandated by Federal law and policy guidelines. CA/OCS/L provides copies of approved Certificates of Loss of Nationality (CLNs) to the following Federal agencies pursuant to statutory requirements:

U.S. Citizenship and Immigration Services (USCIS);

Federal Bureau of Investigation (FBI);

Internal Revenue Service (IRS).

In addition, loss-of-nationality cases involving threats against the United States or U.S. officials may also be brought to the attention of the U.S. Secret Service, consistent with the Warren Commission recommendations. (See 7 FAM 1245.)

7 FAM 1242 DEPARTMENT OF HOMELAND SECURITY, U.S. CITIZENSHIP AND IMMIGRATION SERVICES (DHS/USCIS)

(CT:CON-407; 06-29-2012)

CA/OCS/L provides copies of all approved CLNs to the U.S. Citizenship and Immigration Service (USCIS) under INA 358 (8 U.S.C. 1501).

> CLNs are sent to:
> USCIS Records Operations Branch
> Douglas Development
> Corp. Bldg. – 4th Floor
> 111 Massachusetts
> Ave., NW
> Washington, DC 20529

7 FAM 1243 INTERNAL REVENUE SERVICE (IRS), TAXATION AND LOSS OF NATIONALITY

(CT:CON-407; 06-29-2012)

a. CA/OCS/L provides copies of all approved CLNs to the IRS.

CLNs are sent to:

Internal Revenue Service

11511 Roosevelt Blvd. DP: S-607
Philadelphia, PA 19154

26 U.S.C. 6039G(d)(2) provides that the Secretary of State shall provide to the Secretary of the Treasury a copy of each certificate as to the loss of U.S. nationality under INA 358 (8 U.S.C. 1501), which is approved by the U.S. Secretary of State. This includes both findings of loss of nationality due to renunciation of citizenship (INA 349(a)(5) (8 U.S.C. 1481(a)(5)) and findings of loss of nationality under INA 349(a)(1), INA 349(a)(2), INA 349(a)(3), and INA 349(a)(4) (8 U.S.C. 1481).

Consular officers no longer obtain tax information from renunciants as previously required by the Health Insurance Portability and Accountability Act of 1996 (otherwise known as the Kennedy-Kassebaum Bill), Public Law 104-191, signed into law on August 21, 1996. The American Jobs Creation Act of 2004 (AJCA) (Public Law 108-357) made substantial changes to both the tax Section 877 (26 U.S.C. 877) of the Internal Revenue Codes and information reporting rules 26 U.S.C. 6039G that apply to individuals who expatriated or terminated their residency after June 3, 2004.

U.S. citizens and U.S. noncitizen nationals who lose nationality, and legal permanent resident aliens who turn in/abandon their green cards must file a new Form IRS-8854, Initial and Annual Expatriation Information Statement. Form IRS-8854 must be filed directly with the IRS Philadelphia Service Center rather than with a U.S. embassy or consulate. In countries without a reliable mail service, the post may forward the Form IRS-8854 to CA/OCS/L for transmittal to the IRS.

Form DS-4081, Statement of Understanding Concerning the Consequences and Ramifications of Relinquishment or Renunciation of U.S. Citizenship, reflects current guidance regarding tax implications and loss of nationality and IRS requirements that expatriates file Form IRS-8854, Initial and Annual Expatriation Information Statement.

Questions about expatriation and taxation should be directed to the Internal Revenue Service (IRS) or the IRS Web site. Consular officers are not in a position to provide any advice or answer questions concerning these changes.

Publication of names of individuals who have chosen to expatriate in the Federal Register: 26 U.S.C. 6039G provides that not later than 30 days after the close of each calendar quarter, the Secretary of the Treasury shall publish in the Federal Register (Federal Register Advanced Search) the name of each individual losing U.S. citizenship (within the meaning of section 877(a)) with respect to whom the Secretary receives information under the preceding sentence during such quarter. Accordingly, the names of persons losing U.S. citizenship under INA 349 (8 U.S.C. 1481) have been published as Notices in the Federal Register since 1996. This information can be located in the Federal

Register by selecting "Notice" and using the search terms "Chosen to Expatriate" or "6039G."

Direct inquirers to:

IRS Form-8854 Initial and Annual Expatriation Information Statement
IRS 8854 Instructions
IRS Expatriation Tax
IRS Notice 2005-36
IRS Publication 519 U.S. Tax Guide for Aliens
IRS Abusive Off-Shore Tax Avoidance Schemes

7 FAM 1244
FEDERAL BUREAU OF
INVESTIGATION (FBI)

(CT:CON-407; 06-29-2012)

CA/OCS/L provides copies of all CLNs approved under INA 349(a)(5) to the FBI, National Instant Criminal Background Check System (NICS).

Copies of CLNs are sent to:

Federal NICS Liaison Specialist NICS Section
Criminal Justice Information Services Division
FBI West Virginia Complex
Module A-3
1000 Custer Hollow Road
Clarksburg, WV 26306

The Brady Handgun Violence Prevention Act (Brady Act) of 1993, Public Law 103-159, as amended by the NICS Improvement Amendments Act of 2007 (NIAA), Public Law 110-180, 122 Statutes at Large 2559, enacted January 8, 2008, provides that it is unlawful to sell firearms to persons for whom a finding of loss of nationality due to renunciation has been made. Subsequent laws have extended this restriction to the transporting of hazardous materials by renunciants and other activities. The Brady Act also required establishment of the National Instant Criminal Background Check System (NICS) used by Federal firearms licensees (FFLs) to determine immediately by telephone, or other electronic means, whether the transfer of a firearm would be in violation of Federal or State law. See the National Instant Criminal Background Check System Fact Sheet for additional information.

The U.S. Department of State, Bureau of Consular Affairs, Directorate of Passport Services (CA/PPT) and the FBI entered into an interagency agreement (1998 Memorandum of Understanding (MOU)) on the sharing of information concerning renunciants (persons who lose U.S. citizenship under INA 349(a)(5) and 8 U.S.C. 1481(a)(5)). Per the MOU, CA/PPT provided existing Consular Lookout and Support System (CLASS) data to the FBI. CA/OCS/L provides hard copies of subsequently approved CLNs (under INA 349(a)(5)) to the FBI to be put into the National Instant Criminal Background Check System.

Authorities

18 U.S.C. 922(d)(7) Unlawful Acts: Sale or otherwise dispose of firearms or ammunition to renunciant.

18 U.S.C. 922(g)(7) Unlawful Acts: Shipment transport in interstate or foreign commerce, or possess in or affecting commerce, any firearm or ammunition; or to receive any firearm or ammunition which has been shipped or transported in interstate or foreign commerce by renunciant.

FR 68, 86, May 5, 2003: Transporting Hazardous Materials by Renunciants.

FR 70, No. 82, April 29, 2005: Limitations on the Issuance of Commercial Driver's Licenses With a Hazardous Materials Endorsement.

49 CFR 1572.105 Citizenship Status; Credentialing and Background Checks for Maritime and Land Transportation Security.

27 CFR 478.32: Prohibited Shipment, Transportation, Possession, or Receipt of Firearms and Ammunition by Certain Persons.

7 FAM 1245 SECRET SERVICE - WARREN COMMISSION

(CT:CON-449; 03-25-2013)

Consistent with the special reporting procedures recommended by the Warren Commission Report (WCR) on the assassination of President John F. Kennedy (see Appendix 15 WCR and Recommendations 11 and 12 of the Warren Commission Report (Executive Order 11130)), if a would-be renunciant exhibits hostility toward the United States, its government, or officials and shows indications of mental or emotional instability, the consular officer should notify CA/OCS/L (*Ask-OCS-L@state.gov*), which will coordinate with the Passport Services, Office of Legal Affairs and Law Enforcement Liaison Legal Affairs Division (CA/PPT/L/LA), the Office of the Legal Adviser for Consular Affairs (L/CA), the Office of the Legal Adviser for Law Enforcement and Intelligence (L/LEI) and the Bureau of Diplomatic Security (DS) to ensure that pertinent information is relayed to U.S. law enforcement and intelligence authorities as appropriate.

Posts may also report specific credible threat information to the regional security officer (RSO) who will coordinate with the FBI legal attaché and other law enforcement authorities as appropriate.

7 FAM 1246 THROUGH 1249 UNASSIGNED

7 FAM 1250 NATURALIZATION AND OATH OF ALLEGIANCE TO A FOREIGN STATE

(CT:CON-483; 09-10-2013) (Office of Origin: CA/OCS/L)

7 FAM 1251 NATURALIZATION IN A FOREIGN STATE

(CT:CON-285; 03-06-2009)

Introduction and definition of naturalization: Naturalization and taking a foreign oath do not result in expatriation unless the act is voluntary and accompanied by an intent to relinquish United States nationality:

INA 101(a)(23) (8 U.S.C. 1101(a)(23)) defines naturalization as ...

"The conferring of nationality of a state upon a person after birth, by any means whatsoever."

Section 101(a)(c) of the Nationality Act of 1940 defined naturalization as:

"Conferring of nationality of a state upon a person after birth." b. Naturalization as an expatriating act:

INA 349(a)(1) (8 U.S.C. 1481(a)(1)) provides:

"(a) A person who is a national of the United
States whether by birth or naturalization, shall
lose his nationality by voluntarily performing any
of the following acts with the intention of
relinquishing United States nationality:
(1) Obtaining naturalization in a foreign state upon
his own application or upon an application filed by a
duly authorized agent, after having attained the age of
eighteen years."

Section 401(a) of the Nationality Act of 1940 (54 Statutes at Large 1168-
1169; old 8 U.S.C. 801) provided:

"A person who is a national of the United States,
whether by birth or naturalization, shall lose his
nationality by:
(a) Obtaining naturalization in a foreign state, either upon his
own application or through the naturalization of a parent
having legal custody of such person: Provided, however, that
nationality shall not be lost as the result of the naturalization
of a parent unless and until the child shall have attained the
age of twenty-three years without acquiring permanent
residence in the United States. Provided further, that a
person who has acquired foreign nationality through the
naturalization of his parent or parents, and who at the same
time is a citizen of the United States, shall, if abroad and he
has not heretofore expatriated himself as an American
citizen by his own voluntary act, be permitted within two
years from the effective date of this Act to return to the
United States and take up permanent residence therein, and it
shall be thereafter deemed that he has elected to be an
American citizen. Failure on the part of such person to so
return and take up permanent residence in the United States
during such period shall be deemed to be a determination on
the part of such person to discontinue his status as an
American citizen, and such person shall be forever estopped
by such failure from thereafter claiming such American
citizenship."

Section 2 of the Act of March 2, 1907 (34 Statutes at Large 1228)
provided:

"That any American citizen shall be deemed to
have expatriated himself when he has been
naturalized in any foreign state in conformity
with its laws.

And provided that no American citizen
shall be allowed to expatriate himself
when this country is at war."

Terminology: Foreign state procedures for conferring nationality after
   birth may transpire under various terminology such as
   "naturalization," "registration," "declaration," or "reintegration." The
   terminology used is not determinative; the important factors are
   whether the person acquires the foreign nationality after birth and
   whether an application is made. If these factors are present, a
   potentially expatriating act has been performed.

Application for naturalization:

Naturalization can be an expatriating act under INA 349(a) only if the
   individual affirmatively applies for naturalization;

An expatriating act is not committed if a U.S. national acquires the
   nationality of a foreign country by automatic operation of the
   country's law

(e.g., by being the child of a national of that country) and did not take
affirmative action to acquire the other nationality;

INA 349(a)(1) also applies to naturalization upon the application of duly
   authorized agent after attaining the age of 18, but such cases are rare.
   This naturalization is potentially expatriating only if the person
   making the application was authorized to do so by the person being
   naturalized. The laws of a few countries provide that a married
   woman may be naturalized there only upon her husband's petition.
   See 7 FAM 1290 regarding adults lacking mental capacity, including
   mentally retarded adults, whose U.S. citizenship cannot be
   relinquished by a guardian or trustee;

By contrast, Section 2 of the Act of March 2, 1907, did not require an
   application. Naturalization between April 6, 1917, and July 2, 1921,
   did not result in expatriation. Automatic acquisition of the nationality
   of a foreign state by operation of law did not result in expatriation
   unless there was an oral or written declaration or an overt act clearly
   showing acceptance of the other nationality.

7 FAM 1252 TAKING OATH OF ALLEGIANCE TO A FOREIGN STATE

(CT:CON-483; 09-10-2013)

a. INA 349(a)(2) (8 U.S.C. 1481(a)(2)) provides:

> "(a) A person who is a national of the United
> States whether by birth or naturalization, shall
> lose his nationality by voluntarily performing any
> of the following acts with the intention of
> relinquishing United States nationality:
>
> (2) Taking an oath or making an affirmation or other
> formal declaration of allegiance to a foreign state or a
> political subdivision thereof, after having attained the
> age of eighteen years."

Section 401(b) of the Nationality Act of 1940 (54 Statutes at Large 1169; old 8 U.S.C. 801) provided:

> "A person who is a national of the United States,
> whether by birth or naturalization, shall lose his
> nationality by:
>
> (b) Taking an oath or making an affirmation
> or other formal declaration of allegiance to a
> foreign state."

c. Section 2 of the Act of March 2, 1907 (34 Statutes at Large 1228), provided:

> "That any American citizen shall be deemed to
> have expatriated himself ... when he has taken an
> oath of allegiance to any foreign state.
>
> And provided that no American citizen
> shall be allowed to expatriate himself
> when this country is at war."

An oath of allegiance is a statement affirming one's loyalty to a foreign state.

Such a statement may be oral or in writing; it does not have to be under oath although in many instances it is; and it may be a simple statement, or it may be contained in a larger document, of which the oath is only one part. The taking of such an oath is only an expatriating act if it is taken voluntarily after the age of 18 with the intention of relinquishing one's citizenship.

> The statement of allegiance need not be in any particular form. It may be oral or written. Its words and meaning must express actual allegiance or fidelity to the foreign state or subdivision or to its government, sovereign, constitution, prince, or similar concepts. However, a simple pledge to carry out the duties of a certain job (i.e., sometimes referred to as an oath of office), or similar statement, even though subscribed under oath, is not potentially expatriating.

An oath of allegiance to a foreign state is often taken in connection with naturalization, service in the armed forces of a foreign state, or some other act that is also, in itself, potentially expatriating. A finding of loss of nationality, if made, generally results from the principal act, for example, military service, rather than the oath.

An oath or affirmation of allegiance to another state taken while in the United States cannot result in loss of U.S. citizenship until the person establishes a foreign residence. INA 351 (8 U.S.C. 1483) provides that, except as provided in paragraphs (6) and (7) of INA 349(a), no national of the United States can lose United States nationality while within the United States or any of its outlying possessions, but loss of nationality shall result from the performance within the United States of any of the acts or the fulfillment of any of the conditions specified in this chapter of the INA if and when the national thereafter takes up a residence outside the United States and its outlying possessions.

For an oath or affirmation to be potentially expatriating, it must be meaningful. A meaningful oath is one that is required by a foreign state. Such an oath reflects a transfer of allegiance to a foreign state and/or the abandonment of allegiance to the United States. Gillars v. United States, 182 F.2d 962 (DC 1950). An oath or affirmation will be found to be meaningful only if all four of the following criteria are met:

The oath or affirmation is made to an official of a foreign state authorized to receive the oath or affirmation;

The authorized foreign official in fact does receive the oath or affirmation;

The oath or affirmation is made in a manner that is consistent with the foreign state's law; and

The making and receipt of the oath or affirmation alters the affiant's legal status with respect to the foreign state.

NOTE: *For example, a person who has already acquired a foreign nationality may not expatriate herself by swearing an oath of allegiance to that same foreign state because she already owed that state her allegiance, unless the foreign state's law specifically grants her a new right after making the affirmation not already conferred upon by virtue of her prior naturalization.*

*The Department determines on a case-by-case basis whether an oath of allegiance is meaningful for purposes of INA 349(a)(2).

7 FAM 1253 RESPONDING TO INQUIRIES ABOUT NATURALIZATION OR OATH OF ALLEGIANCE CASES

(CT:CON-285; 03-06-2009)

When you receive inquiries about the possible implications of naturalization in a foreign state or taking an oath of allegiance to a foreign state, you may direct inquirers to the brochure entitled "Advice About Possible Loss of U.S. Citizenship and Dual Nationality" which is available on the Department of State Bureau of Consular Affairs Internet Web site.

7 FAM 1254 PROCEDURES

(CT:CON-483; 09-10-2013)

In Vance v. Terrazas, 444 U.S. 252 (1980), the U.S. Supreme Court held that in establishing loss of citizenship, the U.S. Government must prove an intent to surrender United States citizenship, not just the voluntary commission of an expatriating act such as swearing allegiance to a foreign nation. The U.S. Supreme Court disagreed with the U.S. Government's assertion that a meaningful oath of allegiance to a foreign state is highly persuasive evidence of an intent to transfer or abandon allegiance.

b. *In light of Tarrazas, the Department now presumes that U.S. citizens who naturalize as citizens of a foreign state or who declare their allegiance to a foreign state intend, absent evidence to the contrary, to retain their U.S. citizenship (22 C.F.R 50.40(a) and 7 FAM 1222). A U.S. citizen may readily rebut this presumption by either signing the "Statement of Voluntary Relinquishment of U.S. Citizenship" contained in DS-4079 ("Request for Determination of Possible Loss of United States Citizenship") or by executing a written statement under oath indicating that he or she naturalized as a citizen of a foreign state or declared his or her allegiance to a foreign state voluntarily with the intention of relinquishing U.S. citizenship.*

7 FAM 1255 THROUGH 1259 UNASSIGNED

7 FAM 1260 RENUNCIATION OF U.S. CITIZENSHIP

(CT:CON-407; 06-29-2012) (Office of Origin: CA/OCS/L)

7 FAM 1261 INTRODUCTION

(CT:CON-407; 06-29-2012)

A written renunciation of U.S. citizenship (INA 349(a)(5), 8 U.S.C. 1481(a)(5)) before a U.S. consular officer in the form prescribed by the Secretary of State is a very serious decision. Consular officers must inform potential renunciants of the consequences of renunciation and must keep a detailed record of all interactions with the individual as well as all actions taken in furtherance of the renunciation. This is explained in Form DS-4079, Request for Determination of Possible Loss of United State Citizenship, and Form DS-4081, Statement of Understanding Concerning the Consequences and Ramifications of Relinquishment or Renunciation of U.S. Citizenship.

Who may administer oath of renunciation: The oath must be taken in the presence of a U.S. diplomatic or consular officer. Locally employed staff (LE staff), consular associates, consular agents or any other person may not administer the oath. The oath must be taken outside the United States, its territories and possessions. The oath must be in the precise form prescribed by the Secretary of State: Form DS-4080, Oath of Renunciation of the Nationality of the United States.

Renunciation must conform to the precise requirements of INA 349(a) and 22 CFR 50.50 in order to be effective.

Comprehension: When faced with a potential renunciant, a consular officer must make a judgment whether the individual fully understands what he or she is seeking to do, including the consequences such as losing the right to reside in the United States without documentation as an alien. You must also assess whether the person is acting of his or her own free will, without undue influence from others and without reservation. (See 7 FAM 1290 for guidance about minors, incompetents, prisoners, plea bargains, cults and other special circumstances.)

Intent: Execution of the Oath of Renunciation usually is sufficient evidence of intent to lose U.S. nationality. You should, however, report any contemporaneous statements made by a would-be renunciant that alter the meaning of the renunciation or call into question the individual's intent to renounce citizenship. The Department is unlikely to approve a CLN in such a case. You should also report, and CA/OCS/ACS may ask you to look into, other conduct by the individual that creates doubt that the individual intends to give up the rights and privileges of U.S. nationality. Note, however, that subsequent statements that the individual did not intend to lose nationality are not likely to prevent CA/OCS/ACS from approving the CLN or persuade *CA/OCS/L* to vacate the CLN.

Voluntariness: If the individual is operating under actual duress you should not administer the Oath of Renunciation. See 7 FAM 1290 for guidance regarding renunciation and duress.

Renunciation and statelessness: Potential renunciants who do not possess another nationality or a claim to one are nonetheless permitted to renounce U.S. nationality. In doing so the individual becomes stateless. You should explain the extreme difficulties that a stateless individual may encounter trying to establish residency in a foreign country or traveling between countries in order to ensure that the individual understands the consequences of statelessness. See 7 FAM 1215 for additional information about statelessness. If the individual still desires to proceed with the renunciation, you may proceed.

Potential renunciants who claim a right of continuing residence in the United States: Potential renunciants may also express the intention to continue to reside in the United States or its territories and possessions without documentation as aliens. Since this right of residency is a fundamental right that U.S. citizens and nationals possess, potential renunciants who wish to retain this right do not possess the intent necessary for an effective renunciation. Consular officers must not take renunciations from any individual who seeks to retain the right to reside in the United States or one of its territories or possessions. If a potential renunciant understands the loss of the right to residency and chooses to become stateless nonetheless, the consular officer handling the case must allow him or her to do so. See the Renunciation of U.S. Citizenship by Person Claiming a Right of Residence in the United States brochure.

Would-be temporary renunciants: Many foreign countries now require individuals to divest themselves of other nationalities that they may possess before granting them nationality or permitting them to enjoy the benefits nationals receive. Potential renunciants sometimes inquire whether their U.S. citizenship can be held in "suspense" so that they can temporarily claim a benefit, or take up a policy-level position in the government of, a foreign state. The answer is "no." The individual must choose whether he wishes to keep or give up U.S. citizenship permanently. In renouncing U.S. citizenship one is irrevocably giving up all rights and privileges attendant to being a U.S. citizen. U.S. citizens contemplating renunciation for whatever reason should be advised clearly and unequivocally that, if they choose to exercise their right to renounce U.S. citizenship under INA 349(a)(5) (8 U.S.C. 1481(a)) and the Department of State issues a Certificate of Loss of Nationality, such action is final and irrevocable.

7 FAM 1262 INTERVIEW WITH POTENTIAL RENUNCIANT

7 FAM 1262.1 Threshold Questions

(CT:CON-394; 02-09-2012)

When an individual approaches you attempting to renounce U.S. citizenship, you should:
Verify that the potential renunciant is a U.S. citizen
Clear the individual's name in the Consular Lookout and Support System (CLASS)
Review the PIERS and ACS automated systems for any previous case history
7 FAM 1262.2 Initial Interview with Potential Renunciant

(CT:CON-277; 01-05-2009)

Public information: At an initial interview, provide the individual with a copy(ies) of the following brochures available on the Department of State Bureau of Consular Affairs Web site:

Renunciation of U.S. Citizenship;

Renunciation of U.S. Citizenship by Person Claiming a Right of Residence in the United States;

Possible Loss of U.S. Citizenship and Dual Nationality.

Consequences: Explain the serious consequences of renunciation as summarized in Form DS-4081, Statement of Understanding Concerning the Consequences and Ramifications of Relinquishment or Renunciation of U.S. Citizenship.

Reflection: Tell the individual to think over whether he or she truly wishes to renounce U.S. nationality, and, if so, to schedule an appointment for the renunciation ceremony.

7 FAM 1262.3 Site of Renunciation

(CT:CON-277; 01-05-2009)

Setting: Renunciation procedures should always be held at post in a setting that reminds the renunciant of the gravity of the consequences.

U.S. flag: The flag should be present.

Stand and raise right hand: If possible, the renunciant should stand and raise his or her right hand while taking the Oath of Renunciation. This formality and the symbols of the United States underscore that the renunciant is severing all ties of allegiance to the United States and in doing so loses the protections that the U.S. Government provides to citizens and noncitizen nationals.

7 FAM 1262.4 Documentation of Renunciation

(CT:CON-394; 02-09-2012)

Under Federal regulations at 22 CFR 22.1, an administrative processing fee applies to documenting renunciation of U.S. nationality. The fee should not be collected during the initial interview but only after the individual has decided to proceed with the renunciation and has arrived to take the oath of renunciation. The fee should be collected before conducting the ceremony and administering the oath. If a renunciation is undertaken but not approved by the Department, the fee is not refundable.

As prescribed in 7 FAM 1264, you will need two (2) copies of each of the required documents, which are in fact two original sets of documents, each containing the requisite original signature(s). You must first ask the renunciant to read Form DS-4081, Statement of Understanding Concerning the Consequences and Ramifications of Relinquishment or Renunciation of U.S. Citizenship, and indicate that he or she comprehends it. Then, he or she should be requested to sign Form DS-4081.

NOTE: Failure to sign the Form DS-4081 does not prevent the renunciation from going forward, unless the failure to sign is indicative of a lack of intent to relinquish United States citizenship.

Next, the renunciant must read Form DS-4080, Oath/Affirmation of Renunciation of the Nationality of the United States, and then sign it.

You must sign both Form DS-4080 and Form DS-4081 to attest that you witnessed the actions of the renunciant.

In cases where the renunciant does not understand English and witnesses are required, the witnesses should sign Form DS-4082, Witnesses' Attestation Renunciation/Relinquishment of Citizenship.

You, the renunciant, and any witnesses must initial any deletions, amendments or corrections, however minor, in the body of Form DS-4081, Statement of Understanding Concerning the Consequences and Ramifications of Relinquishment or Renunciation of U.S. Citizenship.

No amendments, deletions, or additions are permitted on Form DS-4080, Oath/Affirmation of Renunciation of the Nationality of the United States.

Any statement of reasons for renouncing must be made in a separate affidavit. If the person does not understand English this should also be witnessed.

You must keep a detailed written record of every interaction with the renunciant, and, following the renunciation, must provide a signed Consular Officer's Opinion to CA/OCS/ACS. This opinion should include the consular officer's assessment of the renunciant's state of mind and the reasons given, if any, for desiring to renounce. Such opinions might note if there appeared to be family pressure to renounce, if the individual was likely renouncing for tax purposes, etc. The opinion should also note if the renunciant displays animosity or has spoken threateningly towards the United States. See 7 FAM Exhibit 1226 for a sample Consular Officer Opinion.

See 7 FAM 1220 regarding preparation of the Certificate of Loss of Nationality, entry of the name into the CLASS system, and disposition of evidence of citizenship (passport, naturalization certificate, certificate of citizenship, etc.).

7 FAM 1263 TRANSLATIONS, INTERPRETERS AND WITNESSES

(CT:CON-407; 06-29-2012)

The need for translations, interpreters, and witnesses for renunciations arises when a potential renunciant cannot read or when the renunciant's comprehension of English is in question. Procedures for these situations are as follows:

If the renunciant cannot read but speaks English:

You must read all documents to the renunciant;

The renunciant and two disinterested witnesses (not relatives, friends or associates) must sign all documents in your presence;

If the renunciant can neither read nor speak English but can read or speak another language:

You must contact the Department (*CA/OCS/L*) to request translations of the Statement of Understanding and the Oath of Renunciation or other documents, which may be subject to the availability of funds;

The renunciant and two disinterested witnesses must sign all documents, including the original English documents and the translations;

A disinterested interpreter (this can be U.S. embassy/consulate locally employed staff (LE staff)) (who may also serve as one of the witnesses) must attest in your presence that the renunciant has read and understood all of the documents in the language that he or she understands;

If the renunciant speaks a language other than English but cannot read:

You must contact the Department (*CA/OCS/L*) to request translations of Form DS-4080, Oath of Renunciation of the Nationality of the United States, and Form DS-4081, Statement of Understanding Concerning the Consequences and Ramifications of Relinquishment or Renunciation of U.S. Citizenship or other documents, subject to the availability of funds ;

The renunciant and two disinterested witnesses must sign all documents, including the original English documents and the translations;

A disinterested interpreter (this may be a U.S. embassy/consulate locally employed staff (LE staff)) (who may also serve as one of the witnesses) shall attest in the presence of the consular officer that the renunciant has been read and understood all of the documents in the language that he or she understands.

Copies of translated documents (Statement of Understanding, Oath of Renunciation) in locally spoken languages should be kept at post for future cases of non-English speaking renunciants. LE staff employees may serve both as interpreters and witnesses if they speak the same language or dialect as the renunciant and they are disinterested parties (not relatives, friends or associates). The renunciant may be accompanied by his or her attorney as a witness, but posts should not be telling renunciants to get an attorney to act as a witness.

7 FAM 1264

DISPOSITION OF DOCUMENTS AND DEPARTMENT APPROVAL

(CT:CON-394; 02-09-2012)

7 FAM 1220 provides guidance about preparation of the loss-of-nationality packet and transmittal to the Department.

You should prepare two (2) original signed and sealed copies of the:

Form DS-4083, Certificate of Loss of Nationality of the United States;

Form DS-4080, Oath/Affirmation of Renunciation of the Nationality of the United States;

Form DS-4081, Statement of Understanding Concerning the Consequences and Ramifications of Relinquishment or Renunciation of U.S. Citizenship;

Form DS-4082, Witnesses' Attestation Renunciation/ Relinquishment of Citizenship, to be used only when the person relinquishing or renouncing citizenship does not speak English.

Note: While Form DS-4079, Request for Determination of Possible Loss of United States Citizenship, is not standard for renunciation cases, where there is a question about intent it may prove useful.

7 FAM 1265 RENUNCIATION AND SPECIAL CIRCUMSTANCES

(CT:CON-277; 01-05-2009)

For information regarding loss of nationality of minors, prisoners, persons of questionable mental competence, plea-bargain case, members of cults, and other special circumstances, see 7 FAM 1290.

7 FAM 1266 RENUNCIATION AND TAXATION

(CT:CON-394; 02-09-2012)

If a would-be renunciant indicates a desire to renounce U.S. citizenship to avoid income tax liability, you should inform the person that:

Renunciation may not exempt him or her from U.S. income taxation; and

If the Department of Homeland Security determines that the renunciation is motivated by tax avoidance purposes, the individual will be found inadmissible to the United States under Section 212(a)(10)(E) of the Immigration and Nationality Act (INA 212(a)(10)(E), 8 U.S.C 1182(a)(10)(E)), as amended.

You should advise the person to contact the Office of International Operations of the Internal Revenue Service for further information. See 7 FAM 1243, Internal Revenue Service (IRS), Taxation and Loss of Nationality.

7 FAM 1267 RENUNCIATION AND THE BRADY ACT

(CT:CON-277; 01-05-2009)

The Brady Handgun Violence Prevention Act (Brady Act) of 1993, Public Law 103-159 — Persons Who Renounce U.S. Citizenship Ineligible to Purchase Firearms, provides that it is unlawful to sell firearms to persons for whom a finding of loss of nationality due to renunciation has been made. Subsequent laws have extended this restriction to the transporting of hazardous materials by renunciants and other activities. The U.S. Department of State and the FBI entered into an interagency agreement on the sharing of information concerning renunciants of May 1998 (CA FBI 1998 MOU)—persons who lose U.S. citizenship under Section 349(a)(5) INA. See 18 U.S.C. 922G Unlawful Acts — Sale of Firearms to Renunciants; Federal Register 68, 86, May 5, 2003 Transporting Hazardous Materials By Renunciants. For additional information, see 7 FAM 1244.

7 FAM 1268 CHECKLIST

(CT:CON-394; 02-09-2012)

When an individual approaches a post claiming the desire to renounce his or her U.S. citizenship, you should:

> Confirm the individual's U.S. citizenship.
>
> Counsel the individual about the extremely serious and irrevocable consequences attendant to the renunciation of U.S. citizenship and advise her or him to return to post to renounce citizenship only after having reflected seriously on the matter.

If the individual decides to proceed, have the individual execute Form DS-4079, Request for Determination of Possible Loss of United States Citizenship, Form DS-4080, Oath of Renunciation of the Nationality of the United States, and Form DS-4081, Statement of Understanding Concerning the Consequences and Ramifications of Relinquishment or Renunciation of U.S. Citizenship.

Scan and transmit, using the ACS system, one original paper set of the CLN, the Oath/Affirmation of Renunciation, Statement of Understanding, and consular officer opinion to the appropriate geographic branch in CA/OCS/ACS.

If the CLN is approved, provide an original paper copy to the individual by registered mail. Be sure to include page 2 on appeals procedures.

Follow the guidance at 7 FAM 1220 regarding disposition of the U.S. passport, naturalization certificate, certificate of citizenship, and consular report of birth abroad.

7 FAM 1269 UNASSIGNED

7 FAM 1270
MILITARY SERVICE AND LOSS OF NATIONALITY

(CT:CON-407; 06-29-2012) (Office of Origin: CA/OCS/L)

7 FAM 1271 INTRODUCTION

(CT:CON-285; 03-06-2009)

7 FAM 1222, paragraph a, explains that in light of the U.S. Supreme Court decisions in Vance v. Terrazas (1980) and Afroyim v. Rusk (1967) the Department of State adopted the administrative presumption found in 22 CFR 50.40 that a U.S. citizen/noncitizen national intends to retain U.S. nationality when he or she commits certain expatriating acts. That administrative presumption is in the process of being revised in 22 CFR Part 50, and includes when a U.S. citizen serves as a commissioned or noncommissioned officer of a foreign state, not engaged in hostilities against the United States (INA 349(a)(3), 8 U.S.C. 1481(a)(3)).

INA 349(a)(3) does not require that the person possess the nationality of the foreign state into whose armed services he or she has entered or served.

If a U.S. citizen serves as a commissioned or noncommissioned officer of a foreign state, not engaged in hostilities against the United States, with the intention of relinquishing U.S. citizenship, he or she may execute Form DS-4079, Questionnaire: Information for Determining Possible Loss of U.S. Citizenship, and the consular officer may proceed to develop the loss-of-nationality case in accordance with 7 FAM 1220.

If a U.S. citizen serves in the armed forces of a foreign state or as a commissioned or noncommissioned officer of a foreign state engaged in hostilities against the United States the administrative presumption of intention to retain U.S. citizenship does not apply, and the consular officer should develop the loss-of-nationality case in accordance with guidance provided in 7 FAM 1274. 7 FAM 1275, paragraph c, provides guidance about U.S. citizens serving in paramilitary organizations abroad, engaged in hostilities against the United States as opposed to service in the armed forces of foreign nation-states.

Child soldiers: While INA 349(a)(3) does not include a reference to age, INA 351(b) (8 U.S.C. 1483(b)) provides that "a national who within six months after attaining the age of eighteen years asserts his claim to U.S. nationality, in such manner as the Secretary of State shall by regulation prescribe, shall not be deemed to have lost United States nationality by the commission, prior to his eighteenth birthday, of any of the acts specified in paragraphs (3) and (5) of Section 349(a) of this title." If a case comes to a consular officer's attention of a U.S. citizen "child soldier" serving in the armed forces of a foreign state engaged in hostilities against the United States, the post should immediately bring the matter to the attention of the Department (see 7 FAM 1240).

Recruiting or hiring someone to serve in a foreign military service may constitute a violation of federal criminal law (18 U.S.C. 958 - 18 U.S.C. 960).

7 FAM 1272 HISTORICAL BACKGROUND

(CT:CON-285; 03-06-2009)

The founding fathers did not regard service to a foreign military to be expatriating.

NOTE: On April 25, 1788, Russia's Empress Catherine II appointed American citizen John Paul Jones to the rank of a Russian Navy rear admiral. Jones retained his U.S. citizenship.

Thomas Jefferson's letter of May 2, 1788, to George Washington regarding the appointment states:

"The war between the Russians and Turks has made an opening for our Commodore Paul Jones. The Empress has invited him into her services. She ensures to him the rank of rear-admiral, will give him a separate command and it is understood that he is never to be commanded. She means to oppose him to the Captain Pacha on the Black Sea. He is by this time probably at St. Petersburg. The circumstances did not permit his awaiting the permission of Congress, but he has made it a condition that he shall be free at all times to return to the orders of Congress whenever they shall please to call for him. And also that he shall not in any case be expected to bear arms against France."

On June 1, 1792, Jones was appointed U.S. Consul "to treat with the Bey of Algiers for the release of American captives." Before he was able to take up this position, he died in Paris July 18, 1792, of pneumonia.

Source: Thomas Jefferson to George Washington, May 2, 1788, George Washington Papers at Library of Congress, 1741-1799, Series 4, General Correspondence 1697-1799; Image 790-795; text of reference to John Paul Jones appears at images 792-793. This is available on the CAWeb Intranet American and the Barbary Pirates –America's First Hostages feature.

The American Civil War amnesty, pardon and restoration of citizenship: On May 29, 1865, President Andrew Johnson issued a Proclamation of Amnesty and Pardon to persons who had participated in the rebellion against the United States. There were fourteen excepted classes, though, and members of those classes had to make special application to the President. Persons excluded from the provisions of amnesty and pardon contained in the proclamation were required to execute an amnesty oath of allegiance to the Union. Robert E. Lee executed the oath before a Virginia notary public. The notarized oath of allegiance was forwarded to William H. Seward, Secretary of State but was never forwarded to President Johnson for approval. In 1970, the oath taken by Robert E. Lee was found in old State Department files stored in the National Archives. In 1975, President Gerald R. Ford signed a bill restoring rights of citizenship to Robert E. Lee posthumously.

See ...

National Archives Robert E. Lee's Parole and Citizenship

President Gerald R. Ford's Remarks Upon Signing a Bill Restoring Rights of Citizenship to General Robert E. Lee, August 5, 1975

The Act of 1907 did not provide that service in a foreign military was an expatriating act. Therefore, U.S. citizens who fought in behalf of the allied powers in World War I before the United States entered the war, did not lose U.S. citizenship due to foreign military service, but rather due to taking an oath of allegiance to a foreign state. Those for whom a finding of loss of nationality was made, had their citizenship restored.

See ...

1918 General Consular Instruction 268

Loss of nationality under section 401(c) of the Nationality Act of 1940 (NA) was limited to United States nationals who were also nationals of the foreign country in whose armed forces they served:

Loss of nationality under this statute could not take place while the person was within the United States or any of its outlying possessions (Section 403(a) NA), and no person under 18 years of age was subject to expatriation under its provisions (Section 402(b) NA);

Military service in a foreign state beginning prior to January 13, 1941 (the effective date of the NA), and continuing thereafter did not result in expatriation unless the person concerned could have terminated his service;

If the conditions for his release were so costly as to render it prohibitive, it was held that the person could not voluntarily secure his release from further service;

It was held that service in the armed forces of an unrecognized state could cause loss of United States nationality under Section 401(c) NA. This holding was based on the precise language of section 401(c), which was not understood to require that the foreign state or its government be recognized by the United States;

Service in the armed forces of a foreign state, to result in loss of nationality, must have been voluntarily performed. The fact that a person was conscripted into service did not necessarily result in the conclusion that the act was performed involuntarily.

7 FAM 1273 EXPATRIATING ACT

(CT:CON-285; 03-06-2009)

A U.S. citizen/noncitizen national who committed or commits one of the following acts during the time period indicated below voluntarily and with the intent to lose U.S. nationality will be found by the Department to have lost U.S. nationality:

Relevant statute	Applicable dates (relevant date is date the potentially expatriating act was committed)	Potentially expatriating act
Section 401(c) of the Nationality Act of 1940 (repealed)	On or after January 13, 1941, but prior to December 23, 1952	Entering, or serving in, the armed forces of a foreign state unless expressly authorized by the laws of the United States, if he has or acquires the nationality of such foreign state.
8 U.S.C. 1481(a)(3) (INA 349(a)(3), as originally enacted	On or after December 23, 1952, but prior to November 14, 1986	Entering, or serving in, the armed forces of a foreign state unless, prior to such entry or service, such entry or service is specifically authorized in writing by the Secretary of State and the Secretary of Defense: Provided,
		That the entry into such service by a person prior to the attainment of his eighteenth birthday shall serve to expatriate such person only if there exists an option to secure a release from such service and such person fails to exercise such option at the attainment of his eighteenth birthday.
8 U.S.C.	On or after	Entering, or serving in, the armed

1481(a)(3) (INA 349(a)(3)), as amended	November 14, 1986.	forces of a foreign state if (A) such armed forces are engaged in hostilities against the United States; or (B) such persons serve as a commissioned or noncommissioned officer. This amendment of the statute in 1986 eliminated the provision allowing for approval of the foreign military service by the Secretaries of State and Defense Immigration and Nationality Act Amendments of 1986, Public Law 99-653, § 18(d), 100 Statutes at Large 3658 (amending INA 349(a)(3), 8 U.S.C. § 1481(a)(3)).

7 FAM 1274
SERVICE IN THE ARMED FORCES OF A FOREIGN STATE ENGAGED IN HOSTILITIES AGAINST THE UNITED STATES
(CT:CON-407; 06-29-2012)

The Department of State holds that voluntary service in the armed forces of a foreign state engaged in hostilities against the United States is strong evidence of intent to relinquish U.S. citizenship. In Vance v. Terrazas, the U.S. Supreme Court recognized that intent can be expressed "in words or found as a fair inference from conduct."

When such a case comes to your attention, you should notify the Department (CA/OCS/ACS) by e-mail alert, followed immediately by a formal cable report. CA/OCS/ACS and *CA/OCS/L* will review the matter carefully, in consultation with the Office of the Legal Adviser. Thereafter, the Department will provide further guidance to post regarding development of the case if deemed necessary.

The cable should include the following information about the individual:

Name;

Date of birth;

Place of birth;

How U.S. citizenship was acquired (birth in the United States, derivative claim through birth abroad; naturalization);

Does the person have the nationality of the foreign state?

If so, how and when did the person acquire foreign nationality?

Position in foreign armed forces;

Brief description of duties;

Any statements by the individual regarding intent to retain or relinquish U.S. citizenship;

Contacts or ties to the United States: Did the person have physical presence or ever reside in the United States? Was the person aware of a claim to U.S. citizenship?

The consular section of the U.S. embassy or consulate should inform the legal attaché, the regional security officer and the defense attaché of the case and include consular (CPAS), judicial (KJUS, KCRM) and security and political/military tags (ASEC), (PINR), (PTER) in the reporting cables.

It is important to remember that commission of a potentially expatriating act is not in itself sufficient to strip a U.S. citizen of his citizenship. Consistent with the Supreme Court's constitutional rulings in Afroyim v. Rusk, 387 U.S. 253 (1967), and Vance v. Terrazas, 444 U.S. 252 (1980), 8 U.S.C. 1481(a) (INA 349(a)) provides that expatriation can occur only if the person who performed a potentially expatriating act did so voluntarily with the intention of relinquishing U.S. citizenship. A determination that these latter requirements have been met usually is made only after direct contact with the potential expatriate since such contact facilitates ascertaining the person's specific subjective intent. Loss-of-nationality determinations can only be made on a case-by-case basis, because whether an individual has lost U.S. nationality depends on the specific facts of his or her case and in particular on whether he or she voluntarily performed an expatriating act and had the required intent to relinquish nationality.

7 FAM 1275
WHAT CONSTITUTES "ARMED FORCES" OF A FOREIGN STATE?

(CT:CON-285; 03-06-2009)

Armed forces: The question of what constitutes "armed forces" under Section 401(c) NA was addressed in Di Girolamo v. Acheson (1951, DC Dist Col) 101 F. Supp. 380. The son of a naturalized citizen born in the United States was not expatriated by service in Fascist Militia after reaching majority, since Fascist Militia was not part of Italian army. In re Quintanilla-Montes (1970, BIA) 13 I & N Dec 508, "Sunday marching" and drill for about one hour in Mexico under direction of soldier from regular Mexican Army, over period of approximately one year, during which time no rank was held, no firearms were issued nor instructions given in use of weapons, no uniforms, pay nor allowances of any nature were received, and no food, transportation nor medical services were furnished, did not constitute service in armed forces of foreign state under 8 U.S.C. 1481(a)(3) (INA 349(a)(3).

Unrecognized foreign state: In United States ex rel. Marks v. Esperdy, 315 F. 2nd 673 (1963), the court held that service in the Cuban rebel forces during the Castro revolution fell into the category of service in the armed forces of a foreign state when the revolution succeeded in overthrowing the Batista Government. A person who serves in the rebel force and continues to serve after the rebels form a new government becomes subject to the provisions of this section. Previous consular guidelines (8 FAM 224.3, Interpretations, TL:CP-31, 4/10/1970) provide that "it was held that service in the armed forces of an unrecognized state could cause loss of U.S. nationality under Section 401(c) NA. This is based on the language of the Act that was understood not to require that the foreign state or its government be recognized by the United States.

The holding found support in Hackworth's Digest of International Law, Volume I, which states that "the existence, in fact, of a new state or a new government is not dependent upon its recognition by other states."

Paramilitary organizations as opposed to nation states: In 2004, the Department received inquiries about the possible applicability of INA 349(a)(3) (8 U.S.C. 1481(a)(3)) to U.S. citizens who may have served in paramilitary-terrorist organizations, engaged in hostilities against the United States. The statute appears to have in mind the traditional concept of war between nation states, and not the type of unconventional war envisioned in those inquiries. The Department of State only makes determinations of loss of nationality under certain circumstances. Loss of U.S. nationality may be adjudicated in a number of fora (e.g., in removal proceedings or judicial proceedings in which nationality is a critical fact), depending on who is seeking to establish loss of nationality and whether the individual who may have lost nationality is in the United States and its outlying possessions or in a foreign state.

INA 358 (8 U.S.C. 1501) provides for adjudication of loss of nationality by the Department of State when there is "reason to believe" that an individual who is in a foreign country has lost nationality while in a foreign country. The consular officer's responsibility under Section 358 extends to persons who are within his or her consular district, because consular officers generally only have jurisdiction to take action with respect to persons in their consular districts. See the Vienna Convention on Consular Relations, 21 U.S.T. 77 (entered into force for the United States December 24, 1969), Articles 5 and 6. Moreover, as a practical matter, the consular officer must have personal contact with the individual to formulate a judgment whether the individual had the required subjective intent to relinquish U.S. nationality.

7 FAM 1276 RESERVE DUTY

(CT:CON-285; 03-06-2009)

Only active duty service in a regular or reserve component is potentially expatriating under INA 349(a)(3). If the foreign law requires a reservist to perform periodic training or military duty, that service constitutes active duty service.

7 FAM 1277 DURESS AND CONSCRIPTION

(CT:CON-285; 03-06-2009)

The question of duress resulting in foreign military service caused a great deal of judicial activity during the late 1940's and the 1950's. The cases primarily involved foreign military service by dual nationals in derogation of Section 401(c) of the Nationality Act of 1940.

There appears to have been some initial debate on whether duress could be used as a defense by dual nationals to expatriation under this section of law. All of the cases reviewed arose from conscription in the foreign armed forces, as opposed to voluntary enlistment. Aside from the question of the burden of proof in these actions, which was decided in the military service case of Nishikawa v. Dulles, 356 U.S. 129 (1958), the courts' primary concern was, therefore, with the questions of whether protest of the conscription by the citizen was necessary and whether conscription per se could be considered duress.

The question of whether formal protest of the induction or conscription would be considered necessary to raise the defense of duress was specifically dealt with in the case of Tomasicchio v. Acheson, 98 F. Supp. 166 (D.C. 1951). The U.S. District Court for the District of Columbia concluded that a protest against being drafted into the Italian army would have been futile and a refusal to take the oath would have been equally ineffective. Moreover, if the plaintiff took an oath of allegiance upon being drafted into the Italian Army, he was then a minor and consequently, the taking of the oath did not operate as an expatriation. Other decisions by the courts of the period reached similar conclusions. See Scardino v. Acheson, 113 F. Supp. 754 (N.J. 1953); Yoshiro Shibata v. Acheson (1949, DC Cal) 86 F Supp 1; Serizawa v. Dulles (1955, DC Cal) 134 F Supp 713; Acheson v. Maenza (1953) 92 US App DC 85, 202 F2d 453; Perri v. Dulles (1953, CA3 NJ) 206 F2d 586; Kondo v. Acheson (1951, DC Cal) 98 F Supp 884; Hamamoto v. Acheson (1951, DC Cal) 98 F Supp 904; Federici v. Clark (1951, DC Pa) 99 F Supp 1019; Shigenori Morizumi v. Acheson (1951, DC Cal) 101 F Supp 976; Yoshida v. Dulles (1953, DC Hawaii) 116 F Supp 618; Riccio v. Dulles (1953, DC Dist Col) 116 F Supp 680; Gensheimer v. Dulles (1954, DC NJ) 117 F Supp 836; Hiroshi Okada v. Dulles (1955, DC Cal) 134 F Supp 183; Namba v. Dulles (1955, DC Cal) 134 F Supp 633; Moldoveanu v. Dulles (1958, DC Mich) 168 F Supp 1.

There was also the question of whether a protest to induction must have been made to United States officials, as opposed to the foreign authorities. In Pandolfo v. Acheson, 202 F. 2d 38, the court held that a United States-Italian dual national was not expatriated by his induction into the Italian army despite the U.S. Government's argument that he should have protested to United States officials.

The second major problem, that of conscription alone as proof of duress, has never been completely resolved by the courts. The Courts of Appeal were divided on the question. The Department's position is that conscription will be considered as a factor highly relevant to possible duress, but must be weighed with all the other evidence in the specific case to determine whether duress was in fact present.

The Department advised posts that the Department does not consider a person who was conscripted (as opposed to one who enlisted in the military) must be held as a matter of law to have served involuntarily. One can enter the military by means of conscription but nonetheless have been willing, even eager to serve in the military. On the other hand, one who has been conscripted is in a far better position to assert that such service was involuntary.

With regard to intent, proven conduct of a person who served in the armed forces of a foreign state at war with the United States is reviewed carefully by the Department when considering the issue of intent. Promotion records and the nature of duties performed are given careful consideration. In addition to the questionnaire, written statements by individuals providing greater detail about the events surrounding the potentially expatriating acts are useful. Historical context from posts is also helpful.

7 FAM 1278 AUTHORIZATION OF THE SECRETARY OF STATE AND SECRETARY OF DEFENSE TO ENTER OR SERVE

(CT:CON-285; 03-06-2009)

INA 349(a)(3), as originally enacted (effective December 23, 1952 – November 13, 1986) and Section 401(c) NA make reference to specific written authorization to serve in the armed forces of a foreign state. In practice, it appears that authorization of the Secretary of State or the Secretary of Defense for service of a U.S. citizen in a foreign military has never been granted.

Earlier consular guidelines (8 FAM 225.3, paragraph a (TL:CP-37; 6-20-72) provided that such authorization would not be granted unless such entry or service "is found to be in the national interests of the United States. This authorization will normally be granted only when the United States is at war or during the existence of a national emergency proclaimed by the President." Subsequent consular guidelines (7 FAM 1263, TL:CON-5) provided "Specific written authorization to serve in the armed forces of a foreign state … will not be granted by the Secretary of State unless the service is found to be in the national interest of the United States. Service while the United States is at peace is considered not to be in the national interest because it could create difficulties in our friendly foreign relations with third countries. Authorization to serve will be granted only for service with friendly nations when the United States is at war or during a national emergency proclaimed by the President. In practice, it appears never to have been granted."

Authorization by local draft board does not amount to consent by Secretary of State or Secretary of Defense to enter or serve in armed forces of foreign state under 8 U.S.C. 1481(3) (INA 349(a)(3)) so as to prevent loss of nationality. See In re D---- (1954, BIA) 5 I & N Dec 674.

A 1994 statute (codified at 10 U.S.C. 1060) provides that a retired member of the U.S. armed services may accept employment with, or hold an office or position in, the military forces of a newly democratic nation if the Secretary of Defense or the relevant branch of the armed services and the Secretary of State jointly approve the employment or the holding of such office or position. (See 22 CFR Part 3a.) Within the Department of State, questions about this subject are handled by the Bureau of Political-Military Affairs (PM) and the Office of the Assistant Legal Adviser for Political and Military Affairs (L/PM).

7 FAM 1279 DESERTION FROM THE U.S. MILITARY OR AVOIDANCE OF U.S. MILITARY SERVICE [REPEALED]

(CT:CON-285; 03-06-2009)

8 U.S.C. 1481(a)(8) provided for loss of nationality for deserting the armed forces of the United States at time of war, if and when convicted thereof by court martial and dishonorably discharged. This was declared unconstitutional by the U.S. Supreme Court in Trop v. Dulles, 356 U.S. 86, 78 S. Ct. 590, 2 L. Ed. 2d 630 (1958). The statute was repealed in 1978 in the Immigration and Nationality Act Amendments of 1986, Public Law No. 99-653, § 18(a), 100 Statutes at Large 3658.

INA 349(a)(10) (8 U.S.C. 1481(a)(10)) provided for loss of nationality for departing from or remaining outside of the United States in time of war or period declared by the President to be a period of national emergency for the purpose of evading or avoiding training and service in the armed forces of the United States. An 1865 statute providing for loss of citizenship by draft evaders was repealed in 1940 Legislation, enacted in 1944 and codified in the Act of 1952, prescribed loss of nationality for departing from or remaining outside the United States during time of war or declared national emergency in order to evade or avoid service in the armed forces of the United States

These statutory provisions were declared unconstitutional by the Supreme Court (Kennedy v. Mendoza-Martinez, 372 U.S. 144, 83 S. Ct. 554, 92 L. Ed. 644 (1963) and were repealed by Congress in 1976, Footnote 297, National Emergencies Act of 1976, Public Law No. 94-412, § 501(a), 90 Statutes at Large 1255, 1258. See Senate Report No. 1168, 94th Congress, 2d Sess. 32 (1976), reprinted in 1976 U.S.C.C.A.N. 2288; H.R. Rep. No. 238, 94th Cong., 2d Sess. 15 (1975).

NOTE: On January 21, 1977, President Jimmy Cater granted a Presidential Pardon to those who had avoided the draft during the Vietnam war by either not registering or traveling abroad. See Proclamation 4483 - Presidential Proclamation of Pardon January 21, 1977

7 FAM 1280

LOSS OF NATIONALITY AND TAKING UP A POSITION IN A FOREIGN GOVERNMENT

(CT:CON-449; 03-25-2013) (Office of Origin: CA/OCS/L)

7 FAM 1281 INTRODUCTION

(CT:CON-285; 03-06-2009)

This subchapter addresses the subject of development of loss-of-nationality cases involving persons who:

Have accepted, are serving in, or performing the duties of any office, post, or employment under the government of a foreign state or political subdivision thereof;

Have attained the age of 18; and

Have the nationality of the foreign state or have taken an oath of allegiance to the foreign state.

The U.S. Supreme Court has ruled that a person cannot lose U.S. nationality unless he or she voluntarily and intentionally relinquishes that status (Vance v. Terrazas, 444 U.S. 252 (1980)). The Supreme Court underscored in Vance v.

Terrazas that "expatriation depends on the will of the citizen rather than the will of Congress," and the Department gives great weight to the expressed intent of the individual. However, the Terrazas Court also recognized that intent may be "expressed in words or found as a fair inference from proved conduct," and the Department has taken the view that actions inherently inconsistent with allegiance to the United States may be more probative than words. See 7 FAM 1285 for a fuller discussion of the subject.

The presumption stated in 7 FAM 1222, paragraph a, found in 22 CFR 50.40, that a U.S. citizen/noncitizen national intends to retain U.S. nationality applies when he or she accepts nonpolicy level employment in the government of a foreign state. (See 7 FAM 1285 for a discussion on what constitutes a policy-level position which the Department now construes as meaning a head of a foreign state.)

If a consular officer becomes aware that a U.S. citizen/noncitizen national accepted a nonpolicy-level position in the government of a foreign state and the individual does not advise you that his or her intent was to relinquish U.S. nationality, the administrative presumption of intent to retain citizenship applies. You should:

See 7 FAM Exhibit 1223 and prepare the Consular Officer Attestation of Non-Loss;

Enter case in ACS System; and

Send attestation to Passport Records for filing attached to Form DS-11, Application for a U.S. Passport, Form DS-82, Application for a U.S. Passport by Mail, or Form DS-4085, Application for Additional Visa Pages, or other passport service. If the person is not applying for a passport, use Form DS-4085, which has been modified for this sort of purpose.

If the person indicates that he or she did intend to relinquish U.S. nationality in accepting a nonpolicy-level position in the government of a foreign state, follow the procedures outlined in 7 FAM 1220 for development of a loss-of-nationality case.

The presumption of intent to retain nationality is not applicable to a policy-level job, but that said, the intent to relinquish nationality must always be established, including for a foreign government policy-level position. Much depends on the nature of the position. Many policy-level jobs involve relatively mundane duties, e.g., health, education, etc., which do not have implications for allegiance. Additionally, even higher-level positions with a foreign government may not be inconsistent with loyalty to the United States. In Vance v. Terrazas, the U.S. Supreme Court recognized that intent can be expressed "in words or found as a fair inference from conduct." (See 7 FAM 1285 for a discussion of the Department position that for the purposes of INA 349(a)(4) (8 U.S.C. 1481(a)(4)) a policy level position constitutes a head of a foreign state.) Development of a loss of nationality for a person in such a position is explained in 7 FAM 1286.

7 FAM 1282 AUTHORITIES

(CT:CON-285; 03-06-2009)

INA 349(a)(4) (8 U.S.C. 1481(a)(4)), as amended, provides that a person who is a national of the United States whether by birth or naturalization, shall lose his nationality by voluntarily performing any of the following acts with the intention of relinquishing United States nationality:

"(4)(A): Accepting, serving in, or performing the duties of any office, post, or employment under the government of a foreign state or a political subdivision thereof, after attaining the age of eighteen years if he has or acquires the nationality of such foreign state.

(4)(B): Accepting, serving in, or performing the duties of any office, post, or employment under the government of a foreign state or a political subdivision thereof, after attaining the age of eighteen years for which office, post, or employment an oath, affirmation, or declaration of allegiance is required."

b. The following chart summarizes INA 349(a)(4) and Section 401(d) of the Nationality Act of 1940:

Statute –		
Expatriating Act	Dates of Application	Notes
INA 349(a)(4)(A) (8 U.S.C. 1481(a)(4)(A))	On or after December 23, 1952	Must be a citizen of the foreign state, over the age of 18, when accepting or performing employment.
INA 349(a)(4)(B) (8 U.S.C. 1481(a)(4)(B))	On or after December 23, 1952	Must take an oath, affirmation or declaration of allegiance to the foreign state, over the age 18, when accepting or performing employment.
Section 401(d) NA	On or after January 13, 1941, but prior to December 23, 1952	Must be employment for which only nationals of the foreign state are eligible; no national could be expatriated under the age of 18 in light of Section 403(b) NA.

Employment of an officer of the United States: The United States Constitution (Article I, section 9, clause 8) prohibits the acceptance of civil employment with a foreign government by an officer of the United States without the consent of Congress.

A 1994 statute (codified at 10 U.S.C. 1060) provides that a retired member of the U.S. armed services may accept employment with, or hold an office or position in, the military forces of a newly democratic nation if the Secretary of Defense or the relevant branch of the armed services and the Secretary of State jointly approve the employment or the holding of such office or position. (See 22 CFR Part 3a.) Within the Department of State, questions about this subject are handled by the Bureau of Political-Military Affairs (PM) and the Office of the Assistant Legal Adviser for Political and Military Affairs (L/PM).

7 FAM 1283
POSITION IN THE GOVERNMENT OF A FOREIGN STATE, INTERNATIONAL ORGANIZATION OR POLITICAL ARM OF A PARAMILITARY ORGANIZATION

(CT:CON-449; 03-25-2013)

Employment in an international organization: Employment with an international organization, even if the person is hired as a foreign national, is not potentially expatriating because such organization is not a foreign state.

Unrecognized state: Employment with a foreign state whose government is not recognized by the United States comes within the scope of INA 349(a)(4), provided that the state satisfies the recognized elements for statehood. The existence, in fact, of a new state or a new government is not dependent upon its recognition by other states. Refer all questions regarding statehood and new governments to *Ask-OCS-L@state.gov*.

Employment with the political arm of a paramilitary organization: Employment with such an organization does not come within the scope of INA 349(a)(4) since it is not employment with a foreign state:

However, if the organization becomes the official government of the foreign state, whether recognized as such by the United States or not, the U.S. citizen could come within the scope of INA Section 349(a)(4);

A U.S. citizen engaged in employment with such an organization, not with a foreign state, could come within the scope of INA 349(a)(7), if convicted by a United States court of "committing any act of treason against, or attempting by force to overthrow, or bearing arms against, the United States, violating or conspiring to violate any of the provisions of 18 U.S.C. 2383 or willfully performing any act in violation of 18 U.S.C. 2385 or violating 18 U.S.C. 2384 by engaging in a conspiracy to overthrow, put down, or to destroy by force the Government or the United States, or to levy war against them, if and when he is convicted thereof by a court martial or by a court of competent jurisdiction";

The consular section of the U.S. embassy or consulate should inform the legal attaché, the regional security officer and the defense attaché of the case and include consular (CPAS), judicial (KJUS, KCRM) and security and political/military tags (ASEC), (PINR), (PTER) in any reporting cables regarding any potential INA 349(a)(7) case addressed to the attention of CA/OCS and the Office of the Assistant Legal Adviser for Law Enforcement and Intelligence (L/LEI) and the Office of the Assistant Legal Adviser for Consular Affairs (L/CA).

Employment by Freely Associated States Marshall Islands (RMI), Federated States of Micronesia (FSM) and Palau are exempt from INA 349(a)(4): Section 144(a) of the Compact of Free Association between the United States of America and the Federated States of Micronesia, Republic of the Marshall Islands and the Republic of Palau provides that persons shall not be subject to the provisions of loss of nationality in Section 349 INA, if they are employed by the governments of these independent foreign states (see Public Law 99-239 (RMI and FSM) and Public Law 99-658 (Palau).

7 FAM 1284 PREREQUISITES FOR A FINDING OF LOSS FOR POLICY-LEVEL EMPLOYMENT WITH THE GOVERNMENT OF A FOREIGN STATE

(CT:CON-285; 03-06-2009)

INA 349(a)(4) (8 U.S.C. 1481(a)(4)) establishes two separate and distinct prerequisites, one of which must be satisfied before a particular type of government employment can be considered potentially expatriating.

INA 349(a)(4)(A) provides for loss of nationality by a person who has or acquires the nationality of the foreign state after attaining the age of 18.

INA 349(a)(4)(B) provides for loss of nationality by a person who accepts a position for which an oath of allegiance is required for that employment after attaining the age of 18.

A person may obtain a position with a foreign government without risk of loss of U.S. nationality if neither prerequisite applies; that is, after attaining the age of 18 he or she does not:

Possess the nationality of the foreign state; or

Take an oath of allegiance to the foreign state.

Section 401(d) NA contains the single prerequisite that the employment be employment for which only nationals of the foreign state are eligible. The individual must be a national of the foreign state. Employment must be restricted to nationals of the foreign state; if an alien may hold such a position, even if none were actually employed, the employment is not a potentially expatriating act.

7 FAM 1285 WHAT IS A POLICY-LEVEL POSITION WITH A FOREIGN STATE?

(CT:CON-449; 03-25-2013)

Except in a head-of-state or foreign-minister case, we will not typically consider employment in a policy-level position to lead to loss of nationality if the individual says that he or she did not intend to lose nationality. Each policy-level position case, however, is fully evaluated on a case-by-case basis.

Holding a head-of-state, head-of-government, or foreign-minister position may be incompatible with maintaining U.S. citizenship, although the issue has not been expressly decided by the Department. Under international law, as applied in the United States, a foreign head of state, head of government, or a foreign minister (who is not a local national) enjoys absolute immunity from the criminal, civil and administrative jurisdiction of U.S. law, a status that some believe to be inconsistent with continued allegiance to the United States. However others have expressed a contrary view. There is also an issue as to whether this absolute immunity typically enjoyed by a foreign head of state or head of government would extend to a U.S. citizen or would instead be reduced to a more limited immunity such as "official acts" immunity, as the United States does not surrender jurisdiction over its own nationals. A third factor is whether the authorities of the office would be inherently incompatible with U.S. allegiance. Additional considerations would be whether other conduct of the individual is consistent with retention of U.S. citizenship such as whether the individual continued to travel to and from the United States on a U.S. passport and continued to pay U.S. taxes, and similar indicia of intent. The possible expatriation of a head of state is a complex issue that would need to be coordinated with the Office of the Legal Adviser, including the Offices of the Assistant Legal Adviser for Consular Affairs (L/CA) and the Assistant Legal Adviser for Diplomatic Law (L/DL). Please refer all head-of-state and head-of-government cases to CA/OCS/L (*Ask-OCS-L@state.gov*) because, as noted, sensitive questions regarding the scope of immunity, its applicability to a U.S. citizen, possible waiver of immunity, authorities of the office, and expatriation, arise.

In 1987, a Federal district court upheld the citizenship of a U.S. citizen serving as a member of a foreign legislative body, despite certain statements in the record indicating a transfer of allegiance. The court ruled that Rabbi Kahane's formal declaration to retain citizenship made simultaneously with the expatriating act preserved his citizenship. (See Kahane v. Schultz, 653 F. Supp. 1486 (1987).)

7 FAM 1286
DEVELOPING A LOSS-OF-NATIONALITY CASE FOR SERVICE IN THE GOVERNMENT OF A FOREIGN STATE

(CT:CON-449; 03-25-2013)

If you are presented with a case of a U.S. citizen or dual national who is running for or holds the position of head of a foreign state or foreign government, or other very high-level foreign government position, you must notify your liaison officer in CA/OCS/ACS and CA/OCS/L (*Ask-OCS-L@state.gov*) by email followed by a cable with the following information (if available):

Name;

Date/place of birth;

How U.S. citizenship was acquired;

Does the person have the nationality of the foreign state? If so, how and when did the person acquire foreign nationality?

Position in foreign government;

Description of duties;

If elected or appointed;

Did the position require the taking of an oath of allegiance? If so, provide text of oath; and

Any statements made by the individual regarding intent to retain or relinquish U.S. citizenship.

CA/OCS will prepare an instruction to the post, in coordination with CA/OCS/ACS, CA/OCS/L, L/CA, and the regional bureau. This will include guidance about whether to request the foreign head of state or other very high-level office holder to complete the loss-of-nationality forms outlined in 7 FAM 1212. If the head of the foreign state declines to complete Form DS-4079, Questionnaire: Information for Determining Possible Loss of U.S. Citizenship, intent and voluntariness will be determined based on conduct.

Often, a foreign government demands as a matter of practice, or requires as a matter of law, that a U.S. citizen seeking such a position demonstrate undivided loyalty by renouncing U.S. nationality. In that event the individual must choose whether:

To refuse the job and therefore not give up U.S. citizenship; or

To accept the job with the other government and terminate his or her U.S. citizenship.

The Department generally considers such renunciations to be voluntary because the individual had a free choice between renouncing and not running for, or seeking, political office.

It is not possible to put one's U.S. citizenship "in suspense" to be somehow "reclaimed" upon leaving foreign government employment. Because of potential subsequent claims that the individual never really intended to renounce, or that the act was involuntary, these renunciations must be thoroughly documented.

7 FAM 1287
INQUIRIES FROM U.S. CITIZENS CONTEMPLATING TAKING UP A POSITION IN A FOREIGN GOVERNMENT

(CT:CON-285; 03-06-2009)

Officials at U.S. embassies and consulates and the Department of State in Washington who receive an inquiry from a U.S. citizen/noncitizen national contemplating taking up a high-level policy position with a foreign government may provide copies of the relevant Bureau of Consular Affairs information brochures.

See ...

Advice About Possible Loss of U.S. Citizenship and Seeking Public Office in a Foreign State

Renunciation of U.S. Citizenship

Possible Loss of U.S. Citizenship and Dual Nationality

You should not provide any opinions or assurances as to whether such action will result in loss of U.S. nationality. Also, you should never suggest that a temporary finding of loss of U.S. nationality can be made and later reversed. This is not possible.

7 FAM 1288
DUAL NATIONALS, PRIVILEGES AND IMMUNITIES, AND REQUESTS FOR TEMPORARY SUSPENSION OF U.S. NATIONALITY

(CT:CON-285; 03-06-2009)

The United States does not accept U.S. citizens or U.S. noncitizen nationals as diplomats (including ambassadors) of foreign states. U.S. nationals may serve as diplomats in a foreign mission to the United Nations, if the Department concurs, but not as bilateral diplomats. This is based on longstanding policy founded on Article 8 of the Vienna Convention on Diplomatic Relations (VCDR) regarding nationality of members of the diplomatic mission. These individuals are not eligible for U.S. visas and must enter the United States on a U.S. passport.

U.S. citizens serving as foreign diplomats would be entitled under the VCDR only to "official acts" immunity from jurisdiction. While this would protect them for acts performed in the course of official duties, it is not a bar to all suits. Moreover, they would still have to appear in court to assert this affirmative defense. Thus, "official acts" immunity would not provide immunity for criminal acts or for civil suits in personal matters.

Article 22 of the Vienna Convention on Consular Relations (VCCR) provides that

"consular officers may not be appointed from among persons having the nationality of the receiving state except with the express consent of that state which may be withdrawn at any time." It is not the practice of the United States Government to accept a United States citizen as a consul general heading a career consular post or as any other career consular officer. A career consular officer must be a citizen of the foreign state and must bear an "A-1" visa, which cannot be issued to U.S. citizens.

The Office of Protocol advises that the United States does not accept requests from sending states to prospectively waive privileges and immunity of a dual national diplomatic or consular officer.

If the individual wishes to assume, or remain in, a diplomatic or consular position in the United States, the individual may voluntarily divest himself or herself of U.S. citizenship. Some foreign diplomats elect to renounce U.S. citizenship under these circumstances in order to serve in high-level diplomatic positions to the United States. It is not necessary to renounce U.S. citizenship to take up a position for a foreign government at the United Nations. A dual national or third-country national cannot renounce or relinquish U.S. citizenship temporarily or put his or her U.S. citizenship "in suspense" while, for example, accepting a diplomatic appointment from a foreign government.

As a matter of policy, the Department of State does not permit U.S. diplomats to have the nationality of the state to which they are assigned. The Foreign Service Act of 1980 provides that only U.S. citizens may be appointed to the Service as officers at posts abroad and our chiefs of mission to foreign countries may only hold U.S. nationality.

7 FAM 1289 UNASSIGNED

7 FAM 1290

MINORS, INCOMPETENTS, PRISONERS, PLEA BARGAINS, CULTS AND OTHER SPECIAL CIRCUMSTANCES

(CT:CON-449; 03-25-2013) (Office of Origin: CA/OCS/L)

7 FAM 1291 INTRODUCTION

(CT:CON-285; 03-06-2009)

This subchapter addresses somewhat unusual questions that arise regarding loss of nationality. These are situations that consular officers should bring to the attention of the Directorate of Overseas Citizens Services (CA/OCS) to obtain specific guidance not provided in 7 FAM 1200.

7 FAM 1292
LOSS OF NATIONALITY AND MINORS

(CT:CON-449; 03-25-2013)

Occasionally, CA/OCS or a post abroad will receive an inquiry from the parent of a child born in the United States who acquired U.S. citizenship at birth protesting the "involuntary" acquisition of U.S. citizenship.

Jus soli (the law of the soil) is a rule of common law under which the place of a person's birth determines citizenship. In addition to common law, this principle is embodied in the 14th Amendment to the U.S. Constitution and the various U.S. citizenship and nationality statutes. The 14th Amendment states, in part, that: All persons born in the United States, and subject to the jurisdiction thereof, are citizens of the United States and of the State wherein they reside.

In U.S. v. Wong Kim Ark, 169 U.S. 649 (1898), the U.S. Supreme Court examined at length the theories and legal precedents on which the U.S. citizenship laws are based and, in particular, the types of persons who are subject to U.S. jurisdiction.

Children born in the United States to diplomats accredited to the United States are not subject to U.S. jurisdiction and do not acquire U.S. citizenship under the 14th Amendment or the laws derived from it (see 7 FAM 1111 d (3) and 7 FAM 1100 Appendix J (Under Development)).

Parents or guardians cannot renounce or relinquish the U.S. citizenship of a child who acquired U.S. citizenship at birth.

A minor who was naturalized through naturalization of parent prior to the Nationality Act of 1940 did not lose citizenship unless voluntary transfer of allegiance by the minor was shown. Any such finding of loss of nationality under the Act of 1907 would now be subject to administrative review in light of the U.S. Supreme Court decisions in Afroyim v. Rusk and Vance v. Terrazas. (See 7 FAM 1230.)

Age limitations in the INA: INA 349(a)(1), INA 349(a)(2) and INA 349(a)(4) contain specific provisions limiting their applicability to a person "having attained the age of eighteen years." No finding of loss of nationality may be made for these acts committed by a person under the age of eighteen.

Child soldiers: INA 349(a)(3) does not include a reference to age. If a case comes to a consular officer's attention of a "child soldier" serving in the armed forces of a foreign state engaged in hostilities against the United States, the post should immediately bring the matter to the attention of CA/OCS/L (*Ask-OCS-L@state.gov*) which will confer with the Office of the Assistant Legal Adviser for Consular Affairs (L/CA) and provide the post with specific guidance on how to proceed. The post should include the name of the child, date and place of birth, proof of U.S. citizenship and information available regarding the foreign military service. The e-mail alert should be followed by a formal cable report. (See also 7 FAM 1270.)

NOTE: INA 351(b) (8 U.S.C. 1483) provides that a national who within six months after attaining the age of eighteen years asserts his claim to U.S. nationality, in such manner as the Secretary of State shall by regulation prescribe, shall not be deemed to have lost United States nationality by the commission, prior to his eighteenth birthday, of any of the acts specified in paragraphs (3) and (5) of Section 349(a) of this title."

Renunciation of U.S. citizenship and minors:

Consult CA/OCS/ACS: Whenever you receive a request to renounce from a minor you immediately must contact CA/OCS/ACS. CA/OCS/ACS will not approve a Certificate of Loss of U.S. Nationality (CLN) for a minor without the concurrence of CA/OCS/L, and appropriate consultation with L/CA;

Voluntariness and intent: Minors who seek to renounce citizenship often do so at the behest of or under pressure from one or more parent. If such pressure is so overwhelming as to negate the free will of the minor, it cannot be said that the statutory act of expatriation was committed voluntarily. The younger the minor is at the time of renunciation, the more influence the parent is assumed to have. Even in the absence of any evidence of parental inducements or pressure, you and CA must make a judgment whether the individual minor manifested the requisite maturity to appreciate the irrevocable nature of expatriation. Absent that maturity, it cannot be said that the individual acted voluntarily. Moreover, it must be determined if the minor lacked intent, because he or she did fully understand what he or she was doing. Children under 16 are presumed not to have the requisite maturity and knowing intent;

Interviewing a minor: When conducting the initial interview with a minor and during the renunciation procedure, you should have at least one other person present. The parents and guardians should not be present. As noted, the interview should take place in the presence of the consular officer and a witness, preferably another consular officer, another Foreign Service officer (nonconsular) or locally employed staff (LE staff). You should also explain that upon reaching the age of 18, the minor has a six-month opportunity to reclaim U.S. nationality. See 7 FAM Exhibit 1292, A Sample Letter to Accompany CLN for Minor Renunciants, which should be provided to minor renunciants together with an approved CLN;

Consular officer's opinion: You should fully document every interaction with the minor and explain in your consular officer's opinion the reasons you believe that the minor is, or is not, mature enough and sufficiently knowing to renounce.

7 FAM 1293 MENTAL COMPETENCY

(CT:CON-407; 06-29-2012)

Because loss of U.S. nationality occurs only when a would-be renunciant or person signing a statement of voluntary relinquishment has the legal capacity to form the specific intent necessary to lose U.S. nationality, cases involving persons with established or possible mental incapacity require careful review. This includes mental disability, mental illness, developmental impairment, Alzheimer's disease, and similar conditions. It may also include cases of substance abuse.

A formal finding of mental incompetency by a court of competent jurisdiction, whether in the United States or abroad, precludes a finding that an individual has the requisite intent.

The requisite intent may also be found lacking if there is evidence that due to mental incapacity or impairment the individual does not understand the seriousness of renunciation, including its irrevocable nature and the major consequences that flow from it.

Voluntariness may also be an issue with persons who suffer from mental incapacity or impairment, as such individuals may be especially susceptible to the influence of others.

Parents, guardians and trustees cannot renounce or relinquish the U.S. nationality of a citizen lacking full mental capacity: A guardian or trustee cannot renounce on behalf of the incompetent individual because renunciation of one's citizenship is regarded, like marriage or voting, as a personal elective right that cannot be exercised by another. Should a situation arise of the evident compelling need for an incapacitated person to relinquish citizenship, you are asked to consult CA/OCS/L for guidance.

Importance of reporting consular observations and relevant facts: An individual who behaves irrationally, belligerently or otherwise unusually may give you reason to question whether he or she has the mental capacity to formulate the intent required to lose U.S. nationality and/or whether he or she is subject to undue influence. You should document all the person's actions and behavior and give your impression of his or her ability to understand the nature and consequences of renunciation. You also should observe and document the behavior of any individual who appears to be attempting to influence the individual to renounce.

While you are not making a clinical diagnosis, your description of the individual's demeanor, behavior, statements, and your assessment of the person's mental and emotional state are very important in making a determination whether the person is capable of formulating the intent to lose U.S. nationality and/or is acting voluntarily. This assessment must be sent to the Department (CA/OCS/ACS) as part of your consular officer opinion.

Accepting the renunciation or relinquishment: You may accept the renunciation or voluntary relinquishment of troubled citizens who insist on exercising their right to renounce. Acceptance does not constitute approval which, by statute (INA 358; 8 U.S.C. 1501) can only occur in the Department. If the Department concludes that the facts rebut the presumption of voluntariness, the Department may decline to approve the Certificate of Loss of Nationality. Permitting such a person to attempt to exercise his or her right to renounce may alleviate tension or conflict on the scene, while reporting the circumstances surrounding the act and the person's demeanor will enable the Department to protect the citizenship of such an individual incapable of forming the requisite intent and voluntariness. The person seeking or claiming loss of citizenship has the burden of establishing knowing intent based on a preponderance of the evidence. Involuntariness may also be established by a preponderance of the evidence.

7 FAM 1294
PRISONERS, FUGITIVES AND PLEA AGREEMENTS

7 FAM 1294.1
U.S. Citizens Imprisoned or Under Other Form of Detention Abroad

(CT:CON-407; 06-29-2012)

a. The inherently coercive nature of incarceration and other governmental detention generally is sufficient to rebut the statutory presumption of voluntariness that is required for a renunciation to result in loss of nationality.

Only in the rarest of instances will CA authorize a consular officer to accept the renunciation of U.S. nationality of a U.S. citizen or noncitizen national who is incarcerated or detained by foreign government authorities.

You must report to CA/OCS/ACS any case where a prisoner or detainee indicates a desire to renounce citizenship.

CA/OCS/ACS, with CA/OCS/L and L/CA concurrence, will provide specific instructions.

A prisoner who has renounced may later claim that he or she did not renounce voluntarily, but rather was motivated by the compulsion to avoid deportation, extradition, or imprisonment.

If CA/OCS/ACS authorizes the renunciation to proceed:

You must interview the prisoner/detainee in private so as to avoid any perception or appearance of coercion from prison officials;

If at all possible, the oath should be taken at post and you may need to make arrangements with prison officials, local police and the post's security officer to have the prisoner escorted;

If you cannot make these arrangements for whatever reason, contact the Department (CA/OCS/ACS) for guidance;

Security and your safety are a major concern in prisoner renunciation cases. If a prisoner is dangerous or a flight risk, you may need to make arrangements to administer the renunciation at the prison or at another secure location. Guards may need to be present as well but you must make every effort to keep the potentially coercive effect of their presence to a minimum. This may involve administering the oath within the guards' sight but physically removed from their hearing. You must get the approval of the Department (CA/OCS/ACS) to implement such procedures.

7 FAM 1294.2 Fugitives from Justice

(CT:CON-285; 03-06-2009)

Persons facing criminal charges in the United States or elsewhere may seek to renounce.

They may express a reluctance to come to post for fear of being apprehended by authorities and may request to be permitted to renounce at another location.

You immediately must alert CA/OCS, CA/PPT/L/LE, the RSO and L/LEI to any case in which CLASS or other information received by you indicates the potential renunciant is or may be a fugitive from justice. You must report immediately any case of a U.S. citizen who is the subject of an extradition or deportation request by the United States who inquires about renunciation of citizenship to CA/OCS and L/LEI. (See 7 FAM 1600, Extradition, and 7 FAM 190, Deserters, Stragglers and Fugitives.)

7 FAM 1294.3
Plea Bargain Agreements with U.S. Prosecutors and
Renunciation or Relinquishment of U.S. Nationality

(CT:CON-449; 03-25-2013)

   The terms of a plea agreement between U.S. Federal or State prosecutors and a criminal defendant may include a provision that the person renounce U.S. nationality in exchange for reduced penalties.

   If such a person comes to you seeking to renounce, you must notify CA/OCS/ACS before proceeding. CA/OCS/ACS will coordinate with CA/OCS/L, L/CA, and L/LEI. Issues are raised by such an arrangement that some would liken to banishment when a citizen at birth is involved.

   If authorized by CA/OCS/ACS to proceed, follow the same procedures as with any other potential renunciant. (See 7 FAM 1260.) You should very carefully and fully document the case and, in particular, the facts in support of voluntariness and intent, as the renunciant may claim lack of intent or involuntariness in the future.

   It is not your role to enforce the plea agreement and you should make no comment on it to the renunciant.

   Inter-agency liaison with the U.S. Department of Justice, Federal or State prosecutors will be done by CA/OCS/L *(Ask-OCS-L@state.gov)*, in coordination with L/CA and L/LEI.

See ...

U.S. Department of Justice, Opinion of the Office of Legal Counsel, Voluntariness of Renunciations of Citizenship Under 8 U.S.C. 1481, 8 Opinion of the Office of Legal Counsel 220, September 27, 1984 – Renunciation Undertaken as Part of Agreement with Federal Prosecutors not to Proceed with Denaturalization or Deportation Proceedings if Subjects of Investigation Agreed to Renounce Their U.S. Citizenship

7 FAM 1295
DEFECTORS, DESERTERS AND PERSONS
AVOIDING SELECTIVE SERVICE

(CT:CON-285; 03-06-2009)

You must consult CA/OCS/ACS if you receive a request for renunciation of relinquishment of U.S. citizenship in the case of a defector, deserters or person avoiding Selective Service. Renunciation of U.S. nationality may not affect the obligation that members of the U.S. military are under to complete this service. (10 U.S.C. 504 (b)(1) provides that a person may be enlisted in any armed force if the person is a national of the United States; an alien who is lawfully admitted for permanent residence. The statute also provides notwithstanding paragraph (1), the Secretary concerned may authorize the enlistment of a person not described in paragraph (1) if the Secretary of Defense determines that such enlistment is vital to the national interest.)

Loss of nationality may not affect a person's obligation to register with the Selective Service System. The Selective Service System operates with permanent authorization under the Military Selective Service Act (U.S.C. App. 451; 50 U.S.C. App 460; 32 CFR 1600 – 1699). With few exceptions, all male United States citizens (including dual nationals) and male aliens residing in the United States and its territories (see 9 FAM Appendix H 400) must register within 30 days of their 18th birthday. (See 7 FAM 550.) (See also Jolley v. Immigration and Naturalization Service, 441 F.2d 1245 (1971).)

You should inform potential renunciants who are motivated by the desire to avoid military service that renunciation is not a shield from prosecution for desertion or failure to register in accordance with the law.

7 FAM 1245 provides guidance regarding reporting requirements to the U.S. Secret Service concerning any renunciant or would-be renunciant expressing hostility toward the United States, its government, or officials and shows indications of mental or emotional instability.

See also 7 FAM 190, Deserters, Stragglers and Fugitives.

NOTE: The U.S. Supreme Court declared unconstitutional:

INA 349(a)(10); 8 U.S.C. 1481(a)(10); Section 401(j) Nationality Act of 1940 (NA) - Departing from or remaining outside of the United States in time of war or period declared by the President to be a period of national emergency for the purpose of evading or avoiding training and service in the armed forces of the United States. (Kennedy v. Mendoza-Martinez, 372 U.S. 144, 83 S. Ct. 554, 92 L. Ed. 644 (1963)); and

INA 349(a)(8); Section 401(g) Nationality Act of 1940 (NA) - Deserting the armed forces of the United States at time of war, if and when convicted thereof by court martial and dishonorably discharged (Trop v. Dulles, 356 U.S. 86, 78 S. Ct. 590, 2 L. Ed. 2d 630 (1958).)

7 FAM 1296 CULT MEMBERS OR MEMBERS OF AMERICAN COMMUNITY GROUPS

(CT:CON-449; 03-25-2013)

Summary: Cults are groups of individuals bound together by their devotion to a particular person or idea. Such groups are often led by either one charismatic individual or a very small cadre of people. Identification with the cult can affect an individual's decision making. If a member of a cult seeks to renounce U.S. nationality, you must explore the issue whether undue influence or duress is involved in the decision to relinquish U.S. nationality. See 7 FAM 170, Reporting on American Community Groups Abroad.

Host-government inquiries: A host government may request clarification of U.S. law and policy regarding loss of nationality if a large group(s) of U.S. citizens or noncitizen nationals attempt to renounce their U.S. citizenship and naturalize as citizens of the host country. Such inquiries should be referred to CA/OCS/L (*Ask-OCS-L@state.gov*).

Renunciation and cult members: If you are notified that a number of cult members wish to relinquish U.S. nationality, you should interview privately each member who wishes to renounce his or her U.S. nationality. Preferably, the interviews should take place on different days and without the presence of other cult members in the waiting room or just outside the post. Interviews should take place in the presence of the consular officer and a witness, preferably another consular officer, another Foreign Service officer (nonconsular), or a locally employed staff (LE staff).

Voluntariness: Individuals who commit an act of expatriation because they fear retaliation by the cult leader or the cult if they do not, may not be acting voluntarily. On the other hand, an individual cult member may have independent personal reasons for seeking to renounce. Your consular officer opinion should discuss in as much detail as possible on the nature and depth of the influence of the cult leader/cult on the individual's decision, the consequences the individual fears from the leader or cult if he or she does not renounce (and what the actual consequences are likely to be), and whether the individual has any personal reasons for seeking to renounce.

7 FAM 1297 ATTEMPTS TO RENOUNCE OR RELINQUISH WHILE IN THE UNITED STATES

(CT:CON-407; 06-29-2012)

CA frequently receives letters from individuals in the United States attempting to notify the U.S. Government that they do not consider themselves subject to the United States or the U.S. State of residence. We also receive letters from persons serving prison sentences in the United States who mistakenly believe that if they renounce or otherwise relinquish U.S. citizenship, they will be released from prison in the United States.

CA/OCS/L advises these individuals of the law regarding renunciations in the United States under 8 U.S.C. 1481(a)(6) (INA 349(a)(6)), which provides:

8 U.S.C. 1481(a)(6)

"A person who is a national of the United States whether by birth or naturalization, shall lose his nationality by voluntarily performing any of the following acts with the intention of relinquishing United States nationality –

(6) making in the United States a formal written renunciation of nationality in such form as may be prescribed by, and before such officer as may be designated by, the Attorney General, whenever the United States shall be in a state of war and the Attorney General shall approve such renunciation as not contrary to the interests of national defense."

The Departments of Justice and Homeland Security have not promulgated regulations or procedures regarding renunciation in the United States under INA 349(a)(6), and there is no officer designated by the Attorney General or DHS to take renunciations.

7 FAM 1298 AND 1299 UNASSIGNED

7 FAM Exhibit 1292
A SAMPLE LETTER TO ACCOMPANY CLN FOR
MINOR RENUNCIANTS

(CT:CON-285; 03-06-2009)

Post Letterhead Date
Dear (NAME):

Every U.S. citizen has the right to renounce voluntarily and intentionally his or her citizenship, as you have done. Because this is a very serious decision with consequences that may not have been apparent to you at the time, the law gives persons like yourself who renounced under the age of 18 an opportunity to reevaluate your decision when you reach the age of 18.

Section 351(b) of the Immigration and Nationality Act (8 U.S. Code 1483) allows you to reclaim your U.S. citizenship within 6 months after your 18th birthday. You are advised to make a note of the deadline to reclaim automatically your U.S. citizenship: the deadline is [insert date six months from 18th birthday.] You may do so by going to any U.S. embassy or consulate or passport acceptance facility, execute a passport application and take an oath of allegiance to the United States. Under this law, if you make such a claim, you will be considered as never having renounced your U.S. citizenship.

Just like the decision to renounce your citizenship, the decision to reclaim it is yours alone. No one, including the U.S. Government, any other government, or even your own family can make the decision for you. Please keep this in mind as you consider whether you may want to make a claim of citizenship once you become 18.

The U.S. Government and the Department of State do not wish to influence your decision. We just want to make sure that you know that you have the right to reconsider and "take back" this decision upon reaching the age of 18. Because this is a very important right that you retain, we ask that you keep this letter with your Certificate of Loss of Nationality should you wish to take advantage of this right when you reach the age of 18. The Department of State will also keep a complete record of your renunciation as well as this letter. Please remember that the period to automatically reclaim citizenship expires on [date].

If you have any questions, do not hesitate to contact (NAME) at (phone number). You may also contact the U.S. Department of State, Office of American Citizens Services and Crisis Management at any time. That office can be reached at 202-647-5225.

Sincerely,

SIGNATURE OF CONSULAR OFFICER

TYPED NAME OF CONSULAR OFFICER TITLE OF CONSULAR OFFICER

7 FAM 1200 APPENDIX A
LOSS OF NATIONALITY AND THE EARLY
YEARS OF THE REPUBLIC

(CT:CON-454; 04-15-2013) (Office of Origin: CA/OCS/L)

7 FAM 1210 APPENDIX A SUMMARY

(CT:CON-285; 03-06-2009)

7 FAM 1200 Appendix A provides some historical perspective regarding U.S. law and policy pertaining to loss of nationality in the early years of the Republic. Two points emerge as having deep historical roots:

> That a person has a right to expatriate; and

> That there has been from the beginning a belief that we ought not to treat (a) "native-born" and (b) naturalized U.S. citizens differently.

7 FAM 1200 Appendix H (under development) provides links to historical instructions to consuls about loss of nationality.

It was one of the earliest principles of the foreign and domestic policy of the United States Government that aliens could come to the United States, be naturalized as citizens of this country, and thereafter be considered as absolved from allegiance to the countries of which they had previously been citizens. This was one of the principles involved in our dispute with Great Britain which led to the War of 1812. Under common law, it was generally held that no person could discard his or her nationality and become an alien without the consent of his or her sovereign or government (Shanks v. Dupont, 28 U.S. 242 (1830)). This concept received some acceptance in the United States but was questioned at an early date.

For most of the 19th century and early 20th century, when questions about loss of nationality arose in the United States, it was in the context of the right of expatriation and the protection of naturalized U.S. citizens abroad.

Current U.S. nationality laws do not explicitly address dual nationality, but the U.S. Supreme Court has stated that dual nationality is a "status long recognized in the law" and that "a person may have and exercise rights of nationality in two countries and be subject to the responsibilities of both." See Kawakita v. United States, 343 U.S. 717 (1952). 7 FAM 080 provides guidance on dual nationality and consular protection.

7 FAM 1220 APPENDIX A THE CONSTITUTION

(CT:CON-285; 03-06-2009)

In 1967, the U.S. Supreme Court, in the matter of Afroyim v. Rusk, 387 U.S. 253, noted:

"The Constitution grants Congress no express power to strip people of their citizenship, whether in the exercise of the implied power to regulate foreign affairs or in the exercise of any specifically granted power";

"And even before the adoption of the Fourteenth Amendment, views were expressed in Congress and by this Court that under the Constitution the Government was granted no power, even under its express power to pass a uniform rule of naturalization, to determine what conduct should and should not result in the loss of citizenship."

Fourteenth Amendment to the U.S. Constitution: The first sentence of the Fourteenth Amendment (1868), as construed in Afroyim v. Rusk, 387 U.S. 253, 268 (1967), "[protects] every citizen of this Nation against a congressional forcible destruction of his citizenship'" and that every citizen has "'a constitutional right to remain a citizen . . . unless he voluntarily relinquishes that citizenship."

The Fourteenth Amendment, Section 1 reads: "All persons born or naturalized in the United States and subject to the jurisdiction thereof, are citizens of the United States and the State wherein they reside."

In the matter of Osborn v. Bank of the United States, 9 Wheat. 738, 827, 6 L Ed 204 (1824), the U.S. Supreme Court, speaking through Chief Justice Marshall, declared that:

Congress, once a person becomes a citizen, cannot deprive him of that status: [The naturalized citizen] becomes a member of the society, "possessing all the rights of a native citizen, and standing, in the view of the constitution, on the footing of a native. The Constitution does not authorize Congress to enlarge or abridge those rights. The simple power of the national Legislature, is to prescribe a uniform rule of naturalization, and the exercise of this power exhausts it, so far as respects the individual."

7 FAM 1230 APPENDIX A EARLY LEGISLATIVE ACTIVITY

(CT:CON-285; 03-06-2009)

The parent laws of our citizenship and naturalization laws were the Virginia laws of 1779 and 1782, which were drawn up by Thomas Jefferson and introduced by George Mason. President Thomas Jefferson recommended the enactment of the Federal law of April 14, 1802 upon which our system of naturalization rests. The Virginia law of 1779 is notable because it contained a provision for expatriation in the following terms:

"That whensoever any citizen of this commonwealth shall by word of mouth in the presence of the court of the county wherein he resides, or of the general court, or by deed in writing under his hand and seal, executed in the presence of three witnesses, and by them proved in either of the said courts, openly declare to the same court that he relinquishes the character of a citizen and exercises his natural right of expatriating himself, and shall be deemed no citizen of this commonwealth from the time of his departure."

(Source: Chapter IV, Vol. 10, p. 129, Hening's Statutes at Large.)

(Source: 59th Congress, 2nd Session, House Document No. 326, Letter from the Secretary of State Submitting Report on the Subject of Citizenship, Expatriation, and Protection Abroad, December 18, 1906.)

On three occasions, in 1794, 1797, and 1818, Congress considered and rejected proposals to enact laws which would describe certain conduct as resulting in expatriation. On each occasion Congress was considering bills that were concerned with recognizing the right of voluntary expatriation and with providing some means of exercising that right.

In 1794 and 1797, many members of Congress still adhered to the English doctrine of perpetual allegiance and doubted whether a citizen could, even voluntarily, renounce his citizenship.

By 1818, however, almost no one doubted the existence of the right of voluntary expatriation, but several judicial decisions had indicated that the right could not be exercised by the citizen without the consent of the Federal Government in the form of enabling legislation:

A bill was introduced to provide that a person could voluntarily relinquish his citizenship by declaring such relinquishment in writing before a district court and then departing from the country;

The opponents of the bill argued that Congress had no constitutional authority, either express or implied, under either the Naturalization Clause or the Necessary and Proper Clause, to provide that a certain act would constitute expatriation. They pointed to a proposed Thirteenth Amendment, subsequently not ratified, which would have provided that a person would lose his citizenship by accepting an office or emolument from a foreign government. The bill was finally defeated.

7 FAM 1240
APPENDIX A CIVIL WAR
DEVELOPMENTS

(CT:CON-285; 03-06-2009)

The Enrollment Act of March 3, 1865 - 13 Statutes at Large 487; 38th Congress, Session II, Chapter 78, 79, 1865 contained a provision (Section 21) concerning loss of nationality for deserters from the military and naval service of the United States and for departing the United States with the intent of avoiding any draft into such service. The law provided:

Section 21:

"And be it further enacted, That, in addition to the other lawful penalties of the crime of desertion from the military or naval service, all persons who have deserted the military or naval service of the United States, who shall not return to said service, or report themselves to a provost-marshal within sixty days after the proclamation hereinafter mentioned, shall be deemed and taken to have voluntarily relinquished and forfeited their rights of citizenship and their rights to become citizens; and such deserters shall be forever incapable of holding any office of trust or profit under the United States, or of exercising any rights of citizens thereof;

And all persons who shall hereafter desert the military or naval service, and all persons who, being duly enrolled, shall depart the jurisdiction of the district in which he is enrolled, or go beyond the limits of the United States, with intent to avoid any draft into the military or naval service, duly orders, shall be liable to the penalties of this section.

And the President is hereby authorized and required forthwith, on the passage of this act, to issue his proclamation setting forth the provisions of this section, in which proclamation the President is requested to notify all deserts returning within sixty days as aforesaid that they shall be pardoned on condition of returning to their regiments and companies or to such other organizations as they may be assigned to, until they shall have served for a period of time equal to their original term of enlistment."

In 1867, Congress passed An Act for the Relief of Certain Soldiers and Sailors, 15 Statutes at Large 14, to remove any disability incurred by loss of citizenship due to desertion.

In 1868, two years after the Fourteenth Amendment had been proposed, Congress specifically considered the subject of expatriation. Several bills were introduced to impose involuntary expatriation on citizens who committed certain acts. With little discussion, these proposals were defeated. Other bills, like the one proposed but defeated in 1818, provided merely a means by which the citizen could himself voluntarily renounce his citizenship.

Then in the July 27, 1868 Act Concerning the Rights of American Citizens in Foreign States 15 Statutes at Large 223; 40th Congress, 2nd Session, Chapter 248, 249 1868, Congress enacted legislation declaring that expatriation is a natural and inherent right of all people.

"WHEREAS the right of expatriation is a natural and inherent right of all people, indispensable to the enjoyment of the rights of life, liberty, and the pursuit of happiness; and whereas in the recognition of this principle this Government has freely received emigrants from all nations, and invested them with the rights of citizenship; and whereas it is claimed that such American citizens, with their descendants, are subjects of foreign states, owing allegiance to the governments thereof; and whereas it is necessary to the maintenance of public peace that this claim of foreign allegiance should be promptly and finally disavowed: Therefore,

Be it enacted by the Senate and the House of Representatives of the United States of America in Congress assembled,

Section 1.

That any declaration, instruction, opinion, order, or decision of any officers of this government which denies, restricts, impairs, or questions the right of expatriation, is hereby declared inconsistent with the fundamental principles of this government."

The July 27, 1868 Act Concerning the Rights of American Citizens in Foreign States (15 Statutes at Large 223) provided no method by which the right of expatriation might be exercised and, except for the limited grounds specified in the Act of March 3, 1865, 13 Statutes at Large 487, legislative guidance as to the circumstances in which nationality might be cast off was completely lacking until the Act of March 2, 1907, 34 Statutes at Large 1228.

The primary aim of the July 27, 1868 Act Concerning the Rights of American Citizens in Foreign States (15 Statutes at Large 223) undoubtedly was to safeguard the status of aliens who had become U.S. citizens. The motivating force of this legislation appears to have been public indignation aroused by the treatment of naturalized Irish-Americans who were arrested in Ireland for participation in the Fenian movement and similar cases in Germany.

(Source: Moore, Digest of International Law, Volume III, (1906), page 579-581.)

"Among the naturalized citizens of the United States, in regard to whom the discrimination had been made, were some who had borne arms in defence [sic.] of the United States during the Civil War.

> Her Majesty's Government could conceive "how impossible it would be for the Government of the United States to agree to a denial or abridgement of their right to extend to them the same natural protection and care which the United States extend to native-born citizens of the United States in similar cases." (Mr. Seward,
>
> Secretary of State to Mr. Adams, Minister to England, Diplomatic Correspondence 1866.) The foregoing cases grew out of the Fenian movement. In consequence of the arrest of naturalized Americans on charges connected with this movement, the question of expatriation assumed an acute form. Among the numerous cases arising at that time, the most notable one, historically, is that of Warren and Costello, two naturalized American citizens who were tried and sentenced in Dublin in 1867, for treason-felony, on account of participation in the Jacmel expedition. It was shown that they had come over to Ireland in that vessel and had cruised along the coast for the purpose of effecting a landing of men and arms, in order to raise an insurrection. This incident, together with others, produced an excitement that, as Mr. Seward stated, extended

"throughout the whole country, from Portland to San Francisco and from St. Paul to Pensacola." The subject was discussed in

Congress, and exhaustive reports were made both in the Senate and the House of Representatives on the subject of expatriation."

(Source: 59th Congress, 2nd Session, House Document No. 326, Letter from the Secretary of State Submitting Report on the Subject of Citizenship, Expatriation, and Protection Abroad December 18, 1906, page 10.)

"The immediate occasion which called forth the law was the arrest of certain naturalized citizens by the authorities of their parent countries, chiefly the German States, for nonperformance of military service, and numerous arrests of naturalized citizens of Irish origin in the United Kingdom charged with crimes of a political character."

7 FAM 1250
APPENDIX A SELECTED
SECRETARIES OF STATE
VIEWS ON EXPATRIATION

(CT:CON-285; 03-06-2009)

Mr. Jefferson: In a communication to "Gouverneur Morris", U.S. Minister to France, dated August 16, 1793, Thomas Jefferson, then Secretary of State, made the following statement:

"Our citizens are certainly free to divest themselves of that character by emigration and other acts manifesting their intention, and may then become the subjects of another power, and free to do whatever the subjects of that power may do."

(Source: The Works of Thomas Jefferson in Twelve Volumes. Federal Edition. Collected and Edited by Paul Leicester Ford.)

Mr. Marshall: In an instruction to Mr. Humphreys, U.S. Consul General in Spain, dated September 23, 1800, Secretary of State John Marshall advised:

"The right of naturalizing aliens is claimed and exercised by the different nations of Europe, as well as by the United States. When the laws adopt an individual no nation has a right to question the validity of the act, unless it be one which may have a conflicting title to the person adopted. Spain therefore cannot contest the fact that these gentlemen are American citizens."

(Source: Moore, International Arbitrations, II, 1001 (1896); MS Inst. U. States Ministers, V 383.)

Further, in an instruction to Rufus King, envoy at London, Mr. Marshall stated on September 20, 1800:

"With the naturalization of foreigners no other nation can interfere further than the rights of that other are affected ... consequently those persons who, according to our laws, are citizens, must be so considered by Britain, and by every other power not having a conflicting claim to the person."

(Source: 59th Congress, 2nd Session, House Document No. 326, Letter from the Secretary of State Submitting Report on the Subject of Citizenship, Expatriation, and Protection Abroad, December 18, 1906.)

Mr. Monroe: In a communiqué to Mr. Foster, British Minister, dated May 30, 1812, Secretary of State James Monroe stated:

"Your proffered exertions to procure the discharge of native American citizens from on board British ships of war, of which you desire a list, has not escaped attention. It is impossible for the United States to discriminate between their native and naturalized citizens, nor ought your Government to expect it, as it makes no such discrimination itself. There is in this office a list of several thousand American seamen who have been impressed into the British service, for whose release applications have from time to time been already made; of this list a copy shall be forwarded to you, to take advantage of any good offices you may be able to render."

(Source: 3 Moore, International Law Digest (1906) 563.)

Mr. Adams: In an instruction to Mr. Shaler, American Consul General at Algiers, dated January 13, 1818, Secretary of State John Quincy Adams, in declining to extend the protection of the United States to a native of Italy who has established himself in Tunis immediately or shortly after procuring naturalization in this country, said:

"Without recurring to the litigious question, how far his rights as a citizen might be affected in the judicial tribunals of this country, by such a long and continued absence following almost immediately after his naturalization, it must be obvious that the obligations of the United States to protect and defend the interests of such a person, in controversies originating in foreign countries, and against the rights of their jurisdiction, cannot be supposed to bind them to the same extent at which it might be proper to interpose in behalf of our resident or native citizens."

(Source: 3 Moore, International Law Digest (1906) 735-736.)

> Mr. Calhoun: In a communiqué to Mr. Pageot, French Minister, dated November 30, 1844, Secretary of State Calhoun stated:

"From these provisions [of the naturalization laws] it would seem by necessary implication, that our laws presuppose a right on the part of citizens and subjects of foreign powers to expatriate themselves and transfer their allegiance, and, although the abstract right has not to my knowledge been settled by any authoritative decision, I feel no difficulty in expressing the opinion that the United States, acting upon these principles in reference to the citizens and subjects of other countries, would not deny their application to cases of naturalization of their own citizens by foreign powers, and, of course, to the case of Demerlier, who, if he should be naturalized by France, would on this view of the subject, be absolved from his allegiance to the United States."

(Source: 3 Moore, International Law Digest (1906) 565.)

> Mr. Buchanan: In a letter to Mr. Rosset, dated November 25, 1845, Secretary of State James Buchanan stated:

"The fact of your having become a citizen of the United States has the effect of entitling you to the same protection from this Government that a native citizen would receive."

(Source: 3 Moore, Digest of International Law (1906) 566.)

Further, Mr. Buchanan stated in a letter to Mr. Huesman, dated March 10, 1847:

> "The Government of the United States affords equal protection to all our citizens, whether naturalized or native, and this Department makes no distinction between the one and the other in granting passports.

It is right to inform you, however, that difficulties have arisen in cases similar to yours. In more than one instance European governments have attempted to punish our naturalized citizens, who had returned to their native country, for military offenses committed before their emigration. In every such case, the Government has interposed, I believe successfully, for their relief, but still they have in the meantime been subjected to much inconvenience. Under these circumstances I could not advise you to incur the risk of returning to Oldenburg, if the business which calls for your presence can be transacted by any other person."

(Source: 3 Moore, Digest International Law (1906) 566.)

And in a communiqué to Mr. Bancroft, Minister to England, dated October 28, 1848, Mr. Buchanan further stated:

"Whenever the occasion may require it, you will resist the British doctrine of perpetual allegiance, and maintain the American principle that British native born subjects, after they have been naturalized under our laws, are, to all intents and purposes, as much American citizens, and entitled to the same degree of protection, as though they had been born in the United States."

(Source: 3 Moore, Digest of International Law (1906) 566.)

And in a further communiqué to Mr. Bancroft, dated December 18, 1848, Mr. Buchanan stated:

"Our obligation to protect both these classes [naturalized and native American citizens] is in all respects equal. We can recognize no difference between the one and the other, nor can we permit this to be done by any foreign government, without protesting and remonstrating against it in the strongest terms. The subjects of other countries, who, from choice, have abandoned their native land, and, accepting the invitation which our laws present, have emigrated to the United States and become American citizens, are entitled to the very same rights and privileges, as if they had been born in the country. To treat them in a different manner, would be a violation of our plighted faith, as well as of our solemn duty."

(Source: 3 Moore, Digest of International Law (1906) 566-567.)

7 FAM 1260
APPENDIX A EARLY OPINIONS OF THE ATTORNEY
GENERAL ON LOSS OF NATIONALITY

(CT:CON-285; 03-06-2009)

In 1856, the Department of State submitted to Mr. Cushing, as Attorney General, the following question propounded by the Bavarian Minister at Berlin:

"Whether, according to the laws of the United States, a citizen thereof, when he desires to expatriate himself, needs to ask either from the Government of the United States, or of the State of which he is the immediate citizen, permission to emigrate; and if so, what are the penalties of contravention of the law." The
Attorney General advised the Secretary of State, in part, that:

"Citizens of the United States possess the right of voluntary expatriation, subject to such limitations, in the interest of the State, as the law of nations or acts of Congress may impose."

(Source: 8 Op. Atty. Gen. 139 (1856))

"Further, Mr. Cushing, after averting to the fact that the National Government had not undertaken to formalize any general law either or citizenship or of emigration, referred to the laws of Virginia, which required, he said, as conditions of the relinquishment of citizenship, (1) a solemn declaration of intention to emigrate, with actual emigration and (2) the assumption in good faith of a foreign allegiance, but declared (3) that the act of expatriation should have no effect if done while in the State or the United States was at war with a foreign power, nor could a citizen of Virginia by emigration discharge himself from any obligation to the State, the nonperformance of which involved by its laws any penal consequence." (3 Moore, Digest International Law (1906) 570.)

On August 17, 1857, Attorney General Jeremiah S. Black wrote to the Secretary of State an opinion regarding expatriation in the matter of Julius Amther, a native of Immelhausen, in Bavaria:

"1. Any citizen of the United States, native or naturalized, may remove from the country, and change his allegiance, provided this be done in time of peace, and for a purpose not directly injurious to the interests of this Government.

If he emigrates, carries his family and effects along with him, manifests his intention not to return, takes up his residence abroad, and assumes the obligation of a subject to a foreign government, this implies a dissolution of his previous relations with the United States, and no other evidence of that fact is required by our law.

A native of Bavaria naturalized in America may return to his native country, and assume his political status as a subject of the King of Bavaria, if there be no law there to forbid it.

4. The Bavarian government may require him to abjure his allegiance to the United States in such form as they may choose to prescribe, since we, on our part, make our own regulations for the admission of Bavarian subjects as citizens of the United States."

(Source: 9 Op. Atty Gen. 62 (1857))

In 1859 Attorney General Black wrote an opinion in the case of Christian Ernst proclaiming in sweeping terms the right of expatriation:

"1. The natural right of every free person, who owes no debt and is not guilty of any crime, to leave the country of his birth, in good faith and for an honest purpose, the privilege of throwing off his natural allegiance and substituting another allegiance in its place, is incontestible.

We take our knowledge of international law, not from the municipal code of England, but from natural reason and justice, from writers of known wisdom, and from the practice of civilized nations; and they are all opposed to the doctrine of perpetual allegiance.

In the United States, ever since our independence, we have upheld and maintained the right of expatriation by every form of words and acts; and upon the faith of the pledge which we have given to it, millions of persons have staked their most important interests.

Expatriation includes not only emigration, but also naturalization.

Naturalization signifies the act of adopting a foreigner and clothing him with all the privileges of a native citizen or subject.

In regard to the protection of our citizens in their rights at home and abroad we have, in the United States, no law which divides them into classes or makes any difference whatever between them."

The Attorney General went on to say:

It was the "natural right of every free person, who owes no
debts and is not guilty of any crime, to leave the country
of his birth in good faith and for an honest purpose, and
to throw off his natural allegiance and substitute another
in its place; that although the common law of England
denied this right, and some of our own courts, misled by
British authority, have expressed, though not very
decisively, the same opinion, this was not to be taken as
settling the question; that natural reason and justice,
writers of known wisdom, and the practice of civilized
nations were all opposed to the doctrine of perpetual
allegiance, and that the United States was pledged to the
right of expatriation and could not without
perfidyrepudiate it."

(Source: 9 Op. Atty. Gen. 356, 357 (1859))

In 1873 Attorney General Williams ruled that the 1868 expatriation
statute's sweeping language also recognized the right of U.S. citizens
to cast off their nationality. The Attorney General indicated that it was
the duty of executive officers to determine if such loss of nationality
had taken place and suggested renunciation and foreign naturalization
as two methods of expatriation. Thereafter the Department of State
assumed the responsibility, in the absence of statute, of determining
whether such loss of nationality occurred.

"The declaration in the act of July 27, 1868, chap. 249, that the right of
expatriation is 'a natural and inherent right of all people,' comprehends our
own citizens as well as those of other countries; and where a citizen of the
United States emigrates to a foreign country, and there, in the mode provided
by its laws, formally renounces his American citizenship with a view to
become a citizen or subject of such country, this should be regarded by our
Government as an act of expatriation.

The selection and actual enjoyment of a foreign domicile, with an intent not to
return, would not alone constitute expatriation; but where, in addition thereto,
there are other acts done by him which import a renunciation of his former
citizenship, and a voluntary assumption of the duties of a citizen of the country
of his domicile, these together with the former might be treated as
presumptively amounting to expatriation, even without proof of naturalization
abroad; though the latter is undoubtedly the highest evidence of expatriation."

(Source: (14 Op. Atty Gen. 295, 296 (1873))

7 FAM 1270 APPENDIX A NATURALIZATION TREATIES

(CT:CON-285; 03-06-2009)

Continuing problems with foreign governments taking legal action against naturalized U.S. citizens lead to the negotiation of a series of naturalization treaties which recognized naturalization as a means of effecting loss of nationality.

Even before the passage of the Act of July 27, 1868, a treaty was negotiated (May 27, 1868) by which the North German Confederation agreed to recognize as Americans former Germans who had secured our naturalization. Soon thereafter similar treaties were negotiated with Bavaria (October 8, 1868); Belgium (July 30, 1869); Hesse (August 7, 1870); Great Britain (September 16, 1870 and May 5, 1871); Austria-Hungary (August 1, 1871); Norway and Sweden (January 12, 1872); and Denmark (April 15, 1873).

(Source: Van Dyne, Citizenship of the United States (1904), Page 327, et seq.)

(Source: 59th Congress, 2nd Session, House of Representatives Document 326 (1906).)

The United States entered into a number of bilateral and multilateral treaties, commonly called the Bancroft Conventions for their chief negotiator, George Bancroft, in the 19th Century and early years of the 20th Century. The treaties provided for loss of citizenship by a citizen of one state upon naturalization in the other state and for loss of the second nationality upon resuming permanent residence in the original country.

From 1868 to 1937, the United States entered into 25 Bancroft treaties covering 34 foreign countries. In the matter of Reid v. Covert, 354 U.S. 1 (1957), the U.S. Supreme Court established that provisions of treaties or executive agreements are unenforceable if they conflict with the Constitution. In Schneider v. Rusk, 377 U.S. 163 (1964), the Supreme Court invalidated a section of the Immigration and Nationality Act of 1952 that purported to strip naturalized Americans of their citizenship after three years' continuous residence in their country of origin; and in Afroyim v. Rusk, 387 U.S. 253 (1967), the Supreme Court, reviewing part of the Nationality Act of 1940, held that Congress has no power to strip anyone of their citizenship, whether it is acquired by birth or by naturalization. These decisions strongly implied that if a case of involuntary loss of citizenship under one of the Bancroft treaties came before the Supreme Court, the expatriation provisions would be found unconstitutional. Concluding that the treaties had become unenforceable, in 1980, the administration of President Jimmy Carter, acting in consultation with the Senate Committee on Foreign Relations, gave notice terminating the treaties to the remaining 21 countries with whom the Bancroft treaties were still in force.

(Source: Borchard, The Diplomatic Protection of Citizens Abroad, page 548 (1928).)

7 FAM 1280 APPENDIX A THE ACT OF MARCH 2, 1907

(CT:CON-454; 04-15-2013)

The provisions of Section 1 of the Act of July 27, 1968, 15 Statutes at Large 223, were incorporated in Section 1999 of the Revised Statutes, as codified in 1878.

On the 13th of April, 1906, the Senate passed a joint resolution providing for a commission to examine the subjects of citizenship of the United States, expatriation, and protection abroad. The Commission consisted of Mr. James B. Scott, Solicitor for the Department of State, Mr. David Jayne Hill, Minister of the United States to the Netherlands, and Mr. Gaillard Hunt, Chief of the Passport Bureau. The findings and recommendations of the Commission were reported to Congress in 59th Congress, 2nd Session, House of Representatives Document 326 (1906). Congress took the recommendations into account in preparing new legislation on expatriation.

The Act of March 2, 1907, 34 Stat. 1228, provided in the first paragraph of section 2 that expatriation would result from the naturalization of an American citizen "in any foreign state in conformity with its laws" or upon his taking an oath of allegiance to any foreign state.

7 FAM 1290
APPENDIX A LATER TWENTIETH CENTURY DEVELOPMENTS

(CT:CON-315; 09-03-2009)

By 1940, the 1907 Act had been repealed, and the Expatriation Act of 1868 was reenacted (8 U.S.C. 800). In 1940, Congress enacted the Nationality Act, 54 Stat. 1137, to codify the nationality laws. The Nationality Act expanded the grounds for loss of nationality to include engaging in military or government service for a foreign government; voting in a foreign political election; formally renouncing citizenship; deserting the armed forces in time of war; treason; and residence for a specified time in foreign countries by naturalized citizens. (Nationality Act of 1940, Sections 401-409.)

Later, Congress enacted the Immigration and Nationality Act of 1952, 8 U.S.C. 1481, 66 Statutes at Large 280, which incorporated the concepts of the Expatriation Act of 1868 and the Nationality Act of 1940 and expanded the grounds for loss of nationality. These later statutes included provisions affecting dual nationals and naturalized citizens (Section 349 INA, Section 350 INA, Section 351 INA and Section 352) discussed in 7 FAM 1200 Appendix C. The current statutory regime is discussed in 7 FAM 1210 and in particular 7 FAM 1214.

While this Appendix reflects the very serious attention given to the issue of the right of expatriation by a young nation populated by immigrants, the United States has come to accept, as reflected in the U.S. Supreme Court's decision in Kawakita v. United States, 343 U.S. 717 (1952), that dual nationality exists, and that when a person who possesses dual nationality travels to the country of his or her other nationality, the person comes within the authority of that nation. The United States will continue to assert our interest in protecting the individual, but, as 7 FAM 080 explains, our ability to do so may be limited. (See also 7 FAM 080 and 7 FAM 416.3.)

The principle that a country shall determine who is a national of that country for purposes of their domestic law is a concept universally recognized under international law.

The United States has recognized the right of expatriation as an inherent right of all people. Citizens of the United States can expatriate themselves through the voluntary performance of a statutorily specified expatriating act with the intention of relinquishing citizenship.

The United States, in accordance with the general principles of international law and practice, objects to the concept of arbitrary deprivation of nationality.

The United States is not a party to the League of Nations Convention on Certain Questions Relating to the Conflict of Nationality Laws, done at The Hague April 12, 1930, registered no. 4137, League of Nations, Treaty Series, volume 179, the U.N. Convention on Stateless Persons (1954), the U.N. Convention on Reduction of Statelessness (1961), or the European Convention on Nationality done at Strasbourg June 11, 1997.

7 FAM 1200 APPENDIX B
U.S. SUPREME COURT DECISIONS ON
LOSS OF NATIONALITY

(CT:CON-407; 06-29-2012) (Office of Origin: CA/OCS/L)

7 FAM 1210 APPENDIX B INTRODUCTION

(CT:CON-285; 03-06-2009)

The United States Supreme Court has considered the issue of loss of nationality many times. Statistically speaking, the Court has agreed to hear a much higher percentage of citizenship cases brought to its attention compared, for example, to criminal or tax law.

7 FAM 1220 APPENDIX B THE NINETEENTH CENTURY

(CT:CON-285; 03-06-2009)

U.S. v. Wong Kim Ark, 164 U.S. 644 (1898). This U.S. Supreme Court case held that Congress had no power to restrict the acquisition of citizenship conferred at birth in the United States; a person born in the United States of Chinese citizen parents was a U.S. citizen under the Fourteenth Amendment and therefore not subject to the Chinese Exclusion Act; and although Wong

Kim Ark could "renounce this citizenship and become a citizen of... any other country," he had never done so. Conduct constituting renunciation of citizenship was not defined. This was the law until the Expatriation Act of 1907 took effect.

7 FAM 1230 APPENDIX B THE 1950'S

(CT:CON-285; 03-06-2009)

On January 9, 1950, in the matter of Savorgnan v. United States et al., 338 U.S. 49 (1950), the U.S. Supreme Court held that a native-born American citizen who, in the United States, became an Italian citizen in 1940, and lived in Italy with her husband from 1941 to 1945, thereby lost her American citizenship even if, when she applied for and accepted Italian citizenship, she did not intend to give up her American citizenship.

On March 31, 1958, the U.S. Supreme Court ruled on three cases regarding loss of nationality. The decisions of that day demonstrated that on loss-of-nationality issues the Supreme Court had abandoned the Savorgnan precepts of the past and that every statute for involuntary expatriation was in jeopardy:

Nishikawa v. Dulles, 356 U.S. 129 (1958). The case involved loss of nationality for service in the armed forces of a foreign state. It concerned a dual U.S.-Japanese citizen who had been held to have lost U.S. citizenship by serving in the Japanese army in World War II. The court deemed it unnecessary to reach the constitutional issue and ruled that the U.S. Government had not established, with the requisite certainty, that the military service was voluntary. The Court held that when the issue of voluntariness is raised, the U.S. Government has the burden of proving the voluntariness of the potentially expatriating act and must do so by clear, convincing, and unequivocal evidence. **Largely as a result of this decision, Congress enacted Section 349(c) INA creating a rebuttable presumption that a potentially expatriating act was performed voluntarily. Congress thereby modified the Court's decision concerning the burden-of-proof requirement in loss-of-nationality cases;**

Perez v. Brownell, 356 U.S. 44 (1958). (SUBSEQUENTLY OVERRULED by Afroyim v. Rusk). This case concerned the loss of nationality by a native born U.S. citizen who had voted in a political election in Mexico. The constitutionality of the statute was upheld, but only by a five-to-four vote. The majority opinion written by Justice Frankfurter extensively reviewed the historical background, finding that the power to prescribe loss of nationality emerged from the power to conduct foreign affairs and the Necessary and Proper Clause of the Constitution. However, since Congress cannot act arbitrarily, there had to be a "rational nexus" or "relevant connection" between such power and the means chosen to effectuate it. Loss of nationality was found to conform to this standard of reasonableness, inasmuch as the termination of the citizenship of a person who becomes involved in the political affairs of a foreign nation reasonably implemented the government's power to conduct foreign affairs. The dissenting opinion of Chief Justice Warren found that "under our form of government, as established by the Constitution, the citizenship of the lawfully naturalized and the native born cannot be taken from them." The Chief Justice recognized that citizenship could be lost by voluntary renunciation or "by other actions in derogation of undivided allegiance to this country." Another dissenting opinion filed by Justice Douglas, with Justice Black concurring, declared that citizenship "may be waived or surrendered, but I see no constitutional method by which it can be taken from him";

Trop v. Dulles, 356 U.S. 86 (1958). In this case the Supreme Court for the first time struck down a loss-of-nationality statute. This statute provided for loss of nationality upon conviction for desertion from the armed forces of the United States during time of war. In this decision the vote was again five-to-four, and Chief Justice Warren's plurality opinion, speaking for the four dissenters in Perez, found this a penal statute, improperly visiting cruel and unusual punishment since it had left the expatriated citizen stateless. Justice Brennan's swing vote was explained in a concurring opinion, concluding that the loss-of-nationality penalty was not rationally related to a demonstrated national need. The four dissenters comprised the remainder of the Perez majority, and found the statute a reasonable and constitutional measure. This rendered Section 401(g) of Nationality Act of 1940 (54 Statutes at Large 1137), as amended, and INA Section 349(a)(x) invalid.

7 FAM 1240
APPENDIX B THE 1960'S

(CT:CON-378; 06-08-2011)

Five years later, in another five-to-four vote, the Court invalidated a statute prescribing loss of nationality as a consequence for evading military service. The majority opinion of Justice Goldberg in Kennedy v. Mendoza-Martinez, 372 U.S. 144 (1963) deemed the statute punitive and found it defective because the penalty was imposed without observing the constitutional safeguards relating to penal sanctions. **This rendered INA Section 349 (a)(10) and Section 401(j) NA unconstitutional.**

The following year another loss of citizenship statute was demolished in Schneider v. Rusk, 377 U.S. 163 (1964). There the law provided for expatriation of a naturalized citizen who resided in his native country for a continuous period of years. A five-to-three majority vitiated INA Section 352 (a)(1) as an invalid discrimination against naturalized citizens. **This rendered INA Section 352 unconstitutional.**

Afroyim v. Rusk, 387 U.S. 253 (1967). The U.S. Supreme Court declared Section 401(e) NA unconstitutional. This section had held that U.S. citizens expatriated themselves by voting in foreign political elections. **Afroyim** went beyond Section 401(e) and established the rule that a U.S. citizen has a constitutional right to remain a citizen "unless he voluntarily relinquishes that citizenship." **Because of this decision, which was retroactive in effect, most of the substantive analysis in loss-of-citizenship cases now requires a judgment as to whether a person intended to relinquish U.S. citizenship at the time of committing the potentially expatriating act. This rendered Section 401(e) of the Nationality Act of 1940, and INA Section 349(a)(6), as originally enacted, unconstitutional under the Fourteenth Amendment. In Afroyim,** the Court overruled Perez v. Brownell, 356 U.S. 44, 2 L. Ed. 2d 603, 78 S. Ct. 568 (1958), and rejected the latter's idea that "Congress has any general power, express or implied, to take away an American citizen's citizenship without his assent."

See 7 FAM 1215 (chart) for a summary of grounds for potential expatriation, including a list of impermissible bases for loss of citizenship invalidated by the Supreme Court.

7 FAM 1250
APPENDIX B 1980: THE TERRAZAS DECISION

(CT:CON-285; 03-06-2009)

In 1980, in the matter of Vance v. Terrazas, 444 U.S. 252 (1980), the U.S. Supreme Court upheld the constitutionality of Section 349(c) INA establishing a rebuttable presumption that a potentially expatriating act was voluntary. The U.S. Government tried to persuade the Court that some voluntary acts are so inconsistent with retention of American citizenship that they may result, automatically, in loss of nationality. The

Court disagreed, noting that "it is difficult to understand that „assent" to loss of citizenship would mean anything less than an intent to relinquish citizenship, whether the intent is expressed in words or is found as a fair inference from proved conduct."

The Court elaborated on its opinion in Afroyim, stating that "the trier of fact must... conclude that the citizen not only voluntarily committed the expatriating act proscribed in the statute, but also intended to relinquish his citizenship."

Under the Afroyim rationale, the Terrazas court added that "one is not free to treat the expatriating acts specified in (the statutes) as the indispensable voluntary assent of the citizen."

The Court concluded: **"In the last analysis, expatriation depends on the will of the citizen rather than on the will of Congress and its assessment of his conduct."**

The Court noted that a person"s intent to relinquish U.S. citizenship could be discerned not only from the person"s words but as a fair inference from proven conduct. The consular officer and the Department perform this latter task in developing loss cases, though as a matter of practice, the Department generally requires a verbal expression of will to relinquish citizenship in order to find loss.

7 FAM 1260
APPENDIX B POST-TERRAZAS: THE 1980'S

(CT:CON-285; 03-06-2009)

In 1985, in Richards v. Secretary of State, Department of State (1985, CA9 Cal) 752 F2d 1413 the U.S. Court of Appeals, 9th Circuit held that Richards'' naturalization in Canada and taking of an oath renouncing all allegiance and fidelity to a foreign sovereign resulted in a knowing loss of citizenship. The Court ruled that "a United States citizen effectively renounces citizenship by performing act that Congress has designated an expatriating act only if he means the act to constitute a renunciation of his U.S. citizenship. In the absence of such an intent, he does not lose his citizenship simply by performing expatriating act, even if he knows that Congress has designated the act an expatriating act. By the same token, we do not think that knowledge of expatriation law ... is necessary, ... and a person who performs an expatriating act with an intent to renounce his US citizenship loses his U.S. citizenship whether or not he knew that act was expatriating act." The Court ruled that Congress is without power to provide that citizens lose their citizenship by mere performance of specified acts; a person loses citizenship if he voluntarily performs an expatriating act enumerated by Congress and if, in performing the act, he intends to relinquish citizenship.

In 1987, in Meretsky v. U.S. Department of Justice, et al., 259 U.S. App. D.C. 487; 816 F.2d 791 (1987), the U.S. Court of Appeals for the District of Columbia upheld the ruling of the District Court, which affirmed the Department of State's issuance of a Certificate of Loss of Nationality ("CLN") against Meretsky, concluding that appellant had voluntarily and intentionally renounced his U.S. citizenship in order to become a citizen of Canada. Meretsky appealed his loss of citizenship to the Board of Appellate Review, which affirmed the State Department's conclusion that Meretsky had performed an expatriating act "with the intent to relinquish citizenship." Meretsky then brought an action in Federal district court under 8 U.S.C. 1503, seeking a declaratory judgment that he had not indeed lost his U.S. citizenship. Finding no material facts in dispute, and on cross motions for summary judgments, on December 30, 1985 the court upheld the issuance of the CLN. The Ninth Circuit rejected an argument that the appellant had become a Canadian citizen to avoid economic hardship, ruling "[t]he cases make it abundantly clear that a person's free choice to renounce United States citizenship is effective whatever the motivation. Whether it is done in order to make more money, to advance a career or other relationship, to gain someone's hand in marriage, or to participate in the political process in the country to which he has moved, a United States citizen's free choice to renounce his citizenship results in the loss of that citizenship."

In 1987, in Kahane v. Shultz (1987, ED NY) 653 F Supp 1486, the U.S. District Court for the Eastern District of New York ruled that a United States citizen with dual citizenship in Israel did not intend to relinquish his U.S. citizenship when he committed expatriating act of accepting a seat in the Israeli Knesset, where acts and statements emphasize beyond doubt that the individual wanted to remain an American citizen, such intent being manifested both before and after he joined Israeli Parliament.

7 FAM 1200
APPENDIX TAKING UP RESIDENCE ABROAD:
LOSS OF NATIONALITY, DUAL NATIONALS AND NATURALIZED CITIZENS
(CT:CON-437; 01-29-2013) (Office of Origin: CA/OCS/L)

7 FAM 1210 APPENDIX C INTRODUCTION

(CT:CON-285; 03-06-2009)

7 FAM 1200 Appendix C provides guidance regarding certain former sections of the Immigration and Nationality Act (INA) which may come to the attention of consular officers and passport specialists due the existence of outstanding lookouts in the Consular Lookout and Support System (CLASS). The sections of law to which these lookouts pertain have been repealed or declared unconstitutional. 7 FAM 1200 Appendix C advises consular officers and passport specialists what to do if you come across one of these cases.

7 FAM 1220 APPENDIX C FORMER INA AUTHORITIES

(CT:CON-285; 03-06-2009)

The sections of law discussed in 7 FAM 1200 Appendix C are:

(1) Former INA 350 (66 Statutes at Large 269) (8 U.S.C. 1482);

NOTE: INA 350 provided for loss of nationality by a dual national by birth (a person who acquired U.S. and foreign nationality by birth) who has voluntarily sought or claimed the benefits of the nationality of any foreign state and thereafter has a continuous residence for 3 years in the foreign state whose nationality he or she acquired at birth at any time after attaining the age of 22. It also provided that nationality is not lost if prior to the expiration of the 3-year period, the national takes an oath of allegiance to the United States before a diplomatic or consular officer and had his or her residence abroad solely for one of the reasons set forth in paragraphs (1), (2), (4), (6), (7), or (8) of INA 353 or paragraph (1), or (2) of INA 354. A further stipulation was that nobody whose foreign residence begins after age 60, and after having his residence in the United States for 25 years after age 18, is subject to loss of nationality under section 350.

(Source 8 FAM 225.11; 4/10/1970.)

Former INA 352 listed the circumstances under which naturalized persons residing abroad would lose their citizenship.

7 FAM 1230 APPENDIX C FORMER INA 350

(CT:CON-437; 01-29-2013)

On October 10, 1978, the President signed Public Law 95-432 which repealed INA 350 effective that date.

The report of the House Committee on the Judiciary reaffirmed that the repeal of the law was prospective.

Pubic Law 95-432 did not restore citizenship to anyone who lost citizenship under Section 350 INA prior to October 10, 1978.

Effective October 10, 1978, anyone who had not completed the three years continuous residence in the foreign state of which he or she was a national at birth was no longer subject to loss of nationality under Section 350 INA.

INA 350 provided for loss of citizenship if a dual national sought or claimed benefits of nationality of a foreign state.

Persons who had acquired U.S. or foreign nationality by naturalization as defined in Section 101(a)(23) INA were not subject to this provision.

The benefits need not actually have been granted; merely seeking or claiming the benefits was contemplated by INA 350. A benefit must have accrued by reason of having the nationality of the foreign country.

A second requirement was that of continuous residence for 3 years in the foreign state of which the person was also a national at any time after age 22. Residence, unlike obtaining the benefit, must have been in the country of the other nationality. INA 101(a)(33) defines "residence" for this purpose. The Bureau of Consular Affairs (CA) considered that the 3-year period of residence began from age 22 or from the date of seeking or claiming the benefit of a foreign state, whichever was later. For example, a person who claimed a benefit at age 25 while residing in the country of the other nationality became subject to INA 350 at age 28. To be subject to that section of law, the person must have retained the other nationality acquired at birth at the time of claiming the benefit and during the 3-year residency period. A person who acquired dual nationality at birth who later lost the other nationality by an act made expatriating by the foreign country's law or by any other procedure was not subject to Section 350.

Persons taking the oath of allegiance within the 3-year period, or whose residence in the foreign state was for the reasons listed in INA 353 and INA 354 were not subject to expatriation regardless of seeking or claiming benefits or later residence.

INA 350 imposed a requirement of voluntariness on the seeking or claiming of a benefit of a foreign state. Persons who did not affirmatively seek the benefit concerned, or had it pressed upon them against their will, were not subject to this section of law.

In light of the Terrazas decision, CA no longer makes a finding of loss of nationality for a person who claimed such a benefit between December 24, 1952 (effective date of the INA) and October 10, 1978 (effective date of Public Law 95-432) who met the 3-year residence requirement, even if he or she claimed that the benefit was sought and obtained with the intention of relinquishing U.S. citizenship.

If a CLASS hit occurs when clearing the name of a passport applicant due to former INA 350, the lookout should be removed and the passport issued.

If a U.S. citizen requests a finding of loss of nationality under former INA 350 the matter should be referred to CA/OCS/L (*ASK-OCS-L@state.gov*).

7 FAM 1240

APPENDIX C SECTION 352 EXPATRIATION AFTER TAKING UP RESIDENCE ABROAD

(CT:CON-285; 03-06-2009)

Former INA 352 listed the circumstances under which naturalized persons residing abroad would lose their citizenship. This section was declared unconstitutional in Schneider v. Rusk, 377 U.S. 163 (1964).

INA 352 was repealed in its entirety by Public Law 95-432 on October 10, 1978.

7 FAM 1200 APPENDIX D
FRAUDULENT NATURALIZATION

(CT:CON-407; 06-29-2012) (Office of Origin: CA/OCS/L)

7 FAM 1210 APPENDIX D INTRODUCTION

(CT:CON-286; 03-18-2009)

As 7 FAM 1200 Appendix A discusses, the founding fathers felt strongly that a person not born in the United States has the right to take U.S. nationality by naturalization and discard the nationality of his or her birth (the right of expatriation).

However, likewise, the early history of the United States reflects the view that a naturalized U.S. citizen who abandons the United States and returns to live in the country of his or her birth, should no longer be regarded as a U.S. citizen.

While the U.S. Supreme Court in the Schneider v. Rusk, 377 U.S. 163 (1964), declared INA 352 and Sections 404 of the Nationality Act of 1940 unconstitutional, they did not strike down INA 340.

7 FAM 1220 APPENDIX D FORMER INA 340(D)

(CT:CON-407; 06-29-2012)

Former INA 340(d) was repealed by the Immigration and Nationality Technical Corrections Act of 1994 (Public Law 103-416)(108 Statutes at Large 4308).

Former INA 340(d) provided that any U.S. naturalized citizen who takes up permanent residence abroad within 5 years after naturalization may have the order admitting that person to citizenship revoked and the certificate of naturalization canceled by court action. Under the statute, the establishment of such permanent residence abroad was prima facie evidence of a lack of intention on the part of such person to reside permanently in the United States at the time of filing the petition for naturalization. This was amended in 1986 (Public Law 99-653) to apply to any U.S. naturalized citizen who took up permanent residence abroad within 1 year after naturalization.

> When instructed by *CA/OCS/L*, consular officers served notice on naturalized U.S. citizens abroad regarding judicial proceedings under former INA 340(d). (See 7 FAM 956.)

7 FAM 1230
APPENDIX D REVISED INA 340

(CT:CON-407; 06-29-2012)

> The revised INA 340(a) (8 U.S.C. 1451(a)) reflects that naturalization may be revoked on the ground that the certificate of naturalization was illegally procured or was procured by concealment of a material fact or by willful misrepresentation.

> INA 340(d) provides that a person shall be deemed to have lost and to lose his citizenship and any right or privilege of citizenship by virtue of revocation of a fraudulent naturalization of such person's parent or spouse through whom naturalization was obtained, regardless of whether such person is residing within or without the United States at the time of revocation.

> Certificates of Loss of Nationality are not prepared for these cases.

> INA 340(d) revocation of naturalization are judicial proceedings.

> Consular officers may be instructed by *CA/OCS/L* to serve notice on naturalized U.S. citizens abroad regarding judicial proceedings under former INA 340. (See 7 FAM 956.)

> U.S. passports cannot be revoked until the individual's U.S. naturalization is revoked. See 7 FAM 1380.

7 FAM 1200 APPENDIX E
LOSS OF NATIONALITY OF MARRIED WOMEN UNDER THE ACT OF 1907 AND SUCCESSOR STATUTES

(CT:CON-454; 04-15-2013) (Office of Origin: CA/OCS/L)

7 FAM 1210 APPENDIX E INTRODUCTION

(CT:CON-253; 04-22-2008)

This Appendix describes the evolution of the adjudication by the Bureau of Consular Affairs (CA) and posts abroad of possible loss of nationality cases involving U.S. citizen women who married aliens in the early part of the 20th century. This guidance is provided because it is pertinent to the adjudication of citizenship claims of the children born abroad to such women.

Frederick Van Dyne, Assistant Solicitor to the Department of State's Treatise on the Law of Naturalization (1907) and Van Dyne's Citizenship of the United States of America (1904) clarify the evolution of U.S. law on this subject.

In an instruction to American Consul Sagua la Grade, June 7, 1894, Acting Secretary Uhl said "The view has been taken by this Department in several cases that the marriage of an American woman to a foreigner does not completely devest [sic.] her of her American citizenship, but that the same is only suspended during coverture, and reverts upon the death of her husband, if she is residing in the United States, or upon her returning to this country if residing abroad." (Van Dyne on Citizenship, 137).

Secretary Sherman, in an instruction to the United States Minister at St. Petersburg, March 15, 1897, said "By our statute an alien wife of an American citizen shares his citizenship. By the usual rules of Continental private international law, a woman marrying an alien shares his status, certainly during his life; but thereafter, on widowhood, reverts to her original status unless she abandons the country of her origin and returns to that of her husband." (Foreign Relations, 1901, 443).

Cockburn, in his work on Nationality (published in 1869, page 24) said: "in every country, except where the English law prevails, the nationality of a woman on marriage merges in that of her husband, she loses her own nationality and acquires his."

Van Dyne also points out that between 1862 – 1877, the Attorney General of the United States issued four different, and sometimes conflicting opinions regarding this issue. During the same period, various U.S. courts and international claims commissions to which the United States was a party issued varying opinions on the subject.

To resolve any doubt that might exist because of the variant decisions of the courts, and opinions of the Secretaries of State and Attorneys General as to the effect of the marriage of an American woman to an alien, on April 13, 1906, the Senate passed a joint resolution providing for a commission to examine the subjects of citizenship of the United States, expatriation, and protection abroad and to make a report and recommendations to the Congress for its consideration. The Citizenship Commission of 1906 recommended and Congress enacted the Expatriation Act of March 2, 1907 (34 Statutes at Large 1228), Section 3, which provided by statute that a female U.S. citizen automatically lost her citizenship upon marriage to an alien.

Section 2, Act of February 10, 1855 (10 Statutes at Large 604) provided "Any women who is now or may hereafter be married to a citizen of the United States, and who might herself be lawfully naturalized shall be deemed a citizen." The Naturalization Act of June 29, 1906 (34 Statutes at Large 596) provided a uniform rule for naturalization.

NOTE: "After 1907, the vast majority of married women in the United States no longer held the status of citizen or non citizen as a consequence of birthplace, parentage, or independent naturalization. The citizenship of their spouse was the single factor ruling their nationalities."

(Bredbenner, A Nationality of Her Own: Women, Marriage and the Law of Citizenship (1998), page 16).

The U.S. Supreme Court upheld the Expatriation Act of March 2, 1907, noting that "the identity of husband and wife is an ancient principle of our jurisprudence." (Mackenzie v. Hare, 239 U.S. 299, 311, 60 L. Ed. 297, 36 S. Ct. 106 (1915). In the matter of Miller v. Albright, 523 U.S. 420 (1998), the U.S. Supreme Court noted:

"The statutory rule that women relinquished their United States citizenship upon marriage to an alien encountered increasing opposition, fueled in large part by the women's suffrage movement and the enhanced importance of citizenship to women as they obtained the right to vote. In response, Congress provided a measure of relief. Under the 1922 Cable Act, marriage to an alien no longer stripped a woman of her citizenship automatically. But equal respect for a woman's nationality remained only partially realized. A woman still lost her United States citizenship if she married an alien ineligible for citizenship; she could not become a citizen by naturalization if her husband did not qualify for citizenship; she was presumed to have renounced her citizenship if she lived abroad in her husband's country for two years, or if she lived abroad elsewhere for five years. A woman who became a naturalized citizen was unable to transmit her citizenship to her children if her non-citizen husband remained alive and they were not separated. See In re Citizenship Status of Minor Children Where Mother Alone Becomes Citizen Through Naturalization, 25 F.2d 210, 210 (NJ 1928) ("the status of the wife was dependent upon that of her husband, and therefore the children acquired their citizenship from the same source as had been theretofore existent under the common law"); see Gettys, The Law of Citizenship in the United States 118 (1934), at 56-57. No restrictions of like kind applied to male United States citizens."

NOTE: The Court referenced: Bredbenner, Toward Independent Citizenship: Married Women's Nationality Rights in the United States: 1855-1937, 54-59 (Ph. D. dissertation, University of Virginia, 1990) and

Sapiro, Women, Citizenship, and Nationality: Immigration and Naturalization Policies in the United States, 13 Politics & Soc. 1, 4-10 (1984).

See...

Bredbenner, A Nationality of Her Own: Women, Marriage and the Law of Citizenship (1998))

National Archives: Women and Naturalization

The Act of March 3, 1931 (46 Statutes at Large 1511), eliminated prospectively loss of nationality by a U.S. citizen woman solely due to marriage to an alien husband.

Legislation in 1936 and 1940 further eroded the Act of 1907, and made provision for resumption of U.S. citizenship, but did not restore U.S. citizenship to all such women. A 1994 amendment to the Immigration and Nationality Act (INA), the Immigration and Nationality Technical Corrections Act of 1994, Public Law 103-416 (108 Statutes at Large 4305), finally provided a remedy, restoring citizenship retroactively and simplifying claims to U.S. citizenship by children of the U.S. citizen women who lost U.S. citizenship under these laws. (See 7 FAM 1270 Appendix E.)

The Department continues to see these cases, which necessitates publication of this Appendix, to explain how these cases were adjudicated, and how they may be remedied today.

7 FAM 1220
APPENDIX E AUTHORITITES

(CT:CON-253; 04-22-2008)

The Act of March 2, 1907 (34 Statutes at Large 1228), Section 3, Expatriation Act;

The Act of September 22, 1922 (42 Statutes at Large 1021), Section 3, Married
Women's Citizenship Act, also known as the Cable Act;

The Act of July 3, 1930 (46 Statutes at Large 854) Naturalization of Married Women;

The Act of March 3, 1931 (46 Statutes at Large 1511), Section 4, Naturalization Act, Amendments;

The Act of June 25, 1936 (49 Statutes at Large 1917), An Act to Repatriate Native-Born Women Who Have Heretofore Lost Their Citizenship By Marriage to An Alien;

The Act of July 2, 1940 (54 Statutes at Large 715), Repatriation of Certain Native-Born Women; and

The Immigration and Nationality Technical Corrections Act of 1994, Public Law 103-416 (108 Statutes at Large 4305).

7 FAM 1230
APPENDIX E EXPATRIATION OF MARRIED WOMEN
PRIOR TO 1907

(CT:CON-253; 04-22-2008)

In the absence of a statute governing the nationality status of a woman national of the United States who married an alien prior to the enactment of the Act of March 2, 1907 (34 Statutes at Large 1228), the Department held that such a woman retained her nationality unless:

> She took up a permanent residence abroad with her husband at some time prior to the passage of the Cable Act on September 22, 1922, and

> She acquired, as a result of marriage, the nationality of the country of which her husband was a citizen or subject.

Such a woman was held to have lost her United States citizenship only if the provisions of both paragraphs (1) and (2) were applicable to her case.

The Executive Order of President Roosevelt of April 8, 1907, amending the diplomatic and consular regulations to reflect the Act of March 2, 1907 on the Expatriation of Citizens and Their Protection (34 Statutes at Large 1228), provided:

"Registration to Resume or Retain Citizenship: When an American woman has married a foreigner and he dies or they are absolutely divorced, in order to resume her rights as an American citizen, she must register with the American consulate within one year after the termination of the marital relation."

Effect of Alien Husband's Naturalization in a Foreign State: An American woman who married a citizen of a foreign state prior to March 2, 1907, and retained her citizenship, but whose alien husband was naturalized in another foreign state before March 2, 1907, was held to have lost her U.S. citizenship if she took up a permanent residence with him abroad prior to September 22, 1922, and acquired the citizenship of the country in which he was naturalized.

7 FAM 1240
APPENDIX E AMERICAN WOMEN MARRIED TO ALIENS BETWEEN MARCH 2, 1907 AND SEPTEMBER 22, 1922

(CT:CON-253; 04-22-2008)

A U.S. citizen woman who married an alien between March 2, 1907 and September 22, 1922, was held to have lost her U.S. citizenship under Section 3 of the Act of March 2, 1907 (34 Statutes at Large 1228).

When she married, on or after September 22, 1922, and prior to March 3, 1931, an alien ineligible to be naturalized as a U.S. citizen, she was held to have lost her U.S. citizenship under Section 3 of the Act of September 22, 1922. It was held that if such a marriage took place between April 6, 1917 and July 2, 1921, during which period the United States was a war, she lost her citizenship as of the termination of World War I if the marital relationship continued after such date and if her husband was still an alien. If, however, the marriage terminated by death or divorce prior to July 2, 1921, or if, in the meantime her husband had become a U.S. citizen, such woman was held never to have lost her status as a U.S. citizen through such marriage.

The Act of March 3, 1931 (46 Statutes at Large 1511), amended Section 3 of the Act of September 22, 1922, so that, thereafter, the provision under which a U.S. citizen woman lost her citizenship solely by marriage to an alien ineligible for U.S. citizenship was eliminated from the Act of September 22, 1922. Thus, a U.S. citizen woman who married any alien on or after March 3, 1931, consequently did not thereby lose her U.S. citizenship solely by reason of Section 3 of the Act of March 2, 1907, (34 Statutes at Large 1228) which provided that U.S. citizen women who married aliens lost their U.S. citizenship.

A U.S. citizen woman who married in the United States lost U.S. citizenship if she later established residence abroad with her husband before September 22, 1922, or March 2, 1931, depending on the eligibility for naturalization of the alien.

7 FAM 1250
APPENDIX E ATTORNEY GENERAL INTERPRETATION OF
THE ACTS OF 1907 AND 1922

(CT:CON-253; 04-22-2008)

On January 25, 1940, Robert H. Jackson, Attorney General of the United States rendered an opinion regarding expatriation of married women (39 Opinion of the Attorney General 411) upholding a finding of loss of nationality of Mrs. A. whose U.S. citizenship was acquired by naturalization by virtue of her marriage to a U.S. citizen in 1894. Mrs. A. was later included in her husband's naturalization as a German citizen with her knowledge in 1924.

On August 22, 1940, Attorney General Robert H. Jackson rendered an opinion regarding loss of citizenship through marriage to an alien (39 Opinion of the Attorney General 474) who acquired naturalization in a foreign state while the United States was at war, that is, between April 6, 1917 and July 2, 1921. The Attorney General's opinion reflected that as these provisions have been construed by the Department of State, the Immigration and Naturalization Service, and by the courts, it has been generally understood that the proviso in section 2 prevented loss of citizenship while the United States was at war. The Solicitor of the Department of Labor (at one time the parent agency of the former INS) concluded in 1938 that the acts of these citizens amounted to attempted expatriation which never became effective. The Legal Adviser of the U.S. Department of State expressed the view in a letter to the Attorney General of July 10, 1940, that expatriation became effective upon termination of the war. The Attorney General concluded that "the preponderance of the judicial determinations in several courts which have dealt with the question impel me to the conclusion that American citizens who were naturalized abroad after entry into the war by this country on April 6, 1917, and prior to the congressional resolution of July 2, 1921, declaring the war at an end, lost their citizenship as of the latter date, and that this is also true of American women who married aliens or who were naturalized abroad through the naturalization of their husbands during the same period, provided the marital status had not previously been terminated."

7 FAM 1260
APPENDIX E RESUMPTION OF NATIONALITY

(CT:CON-253; 04-22-2008)

Pursuant to INA 324(c) (8 U.S.C. 1435(c)) a woman formerly a citizen of the United States at birth who wished to regain her citizenship under INA 324(c) can apply abroad to a diplomatic or consular officer on the form prescribed by the Department to take the oath of allegiance prescribed by section 337 of that Act. The applicant was required to submit documentary evidence to establish her eligibility to take the oath of allegiance. If the diplomatic or consular officer or the Department determined, when the application was submitted to the Department for decision, that the applicant is ineligible for resumption of citizenship because of INA 313 (8 U.S.C. 1424), the oath was not to be administered.

A woman who has been restored to citizenship by the Act of June 25, 1936 (49 Statutes at Large 1917), as amended by the Act of July 2, 1940 (54 Statutes at Large 715), but who failed to take the oath of allegiance prior to December 24, 1952, as prescribed by the nationality laws, can apply abroad to any diplomatic or consular officer to take the oath of allegiance as prescribed by INA 337 (8 U.S.C. 1448).

Upon request and payment of the prescribed fee, a diplomatic or consular officer or the Department issued a certified copy of the application and oath administered to a woman repatriated under this section.

This resumption of citizenship was also called "repatriation", a term which in current consular parlance has a different meaning (see 7 FAM 370).

7 FAM 1270
APPENDIX E EFFECT OF AFROYIM AND TERRAZAS ON SECTION 3 OF THE ACT OF 1907

(CT:CON-407; 06-29-2012)

Marriage of a U.S. citizen woman to an alien is expatriating under Section 3 of the Act of March 2, 1907 (34 Statutes at Large 1228) only if there is a statement by the U.S. citizen woman that she intended to relinquish U.S. citizenship.

If an "L" Consular Lookout and Support System (CLASS) hold exists for loss of nationality in a case involving loss by marriage, the cases should be referred to CA/OCS/L (Ask-OCS-L-Dom-Post@state.gov) for administrative review.

If a "Q" lookout exists in CLASS under this section of law, absent a statement by the U.S. citizen woman that she intended to relinquish U.S. citizenship, the "Q" lookout should be removed by CA/OCS/ACS or passport agency or center.

7 FAM 1280
APPENDIX E THE 1994 AMENDMENT TO THE IMMIGRATION AND NATIONALITY ACT

(CT:CON-454; 04-15-2013)

The Immigration and Nationality Technical Corrections Act of 1994, Public Law 103-416 (108 Statutes at Large 4305), October 25, 1994 (see 7 FAM 1133.2-1) retroactively benefited the children born abroad to U.S. women and alien fathers, prior to May 24, 1934, including those for whom findings of loss of nationality were made under the Acts of 1907 and 1922.

If a post abroad or a passport agency or center receives a passport application for a person born abroad prior to May 24, 1934 to a U.S. citizen mother married to an alien who lost U.S. citizenship under the Act of 1907 and its successor statutes, or for whom a "Q" lookout exists for possible loss of citizenship, follow the guidance in *7 FAM* 1270 Appendix E and 7 FAM 1230 general guidance regarding administrative review and appeal of previous findings of loss of nationality.

The CLASS hold against the mother should be removed prior to issuance of a passport to the child.

7 FAM 1290
APPENDIX E HISTORICAL INSTRUCTIONS REGARDING SECTION 3 OF THE ACT OF 1907

(CT:CON-253; 04-22-2008)

Historical instructions to consuls regarding loss of nationality and married women under the Act of March 2, 1907 and its successor statutes are available on the CA Web Intranet by searching under Citizens Services, Service Area: Loss of Nationality, Reference Materials and Reports.

7 FAM 1200 APPENDIX G
POSTHUMOUS LOSS OF NATIONALITY

(CT:CON-407: 06-29-2012) (Office of Origin: CA/OCS/L)

7 FAM 1210 APPENDIX G INTRODUCTION

(CT:CON-256: 05-15-2008)

In reviewing posthumous loss of citizenship cases, it is important to emphasize that the burden of proof always rests upon the shoulders of the party asserting that a loss has occurred. It is also important to keep in mind that each case needs to be considered on its own merits.

The latter caveat notwithstanding, in instances when a finding of loss has not been made prior to a U.S. citizen's death, the Bureau of Consular Affairs, Directorate of Overseas Citizens, Office of American Citizens Services and Crisis Management (CA/OCS/ACS) would be reluctant to approve a Certificate of Loss of Nationality (CLN) posthumously, and such approvals are in fact rare. Our reticence is due to the fact that we did not have, prior to death, an opportunity to ascertain from the concerned individual whether his/her commission of the statutory act of expatriation was done voluntarily with the intent to relinquish U.S. citizenship.

CA/OCS/ACS could approve a CLN for an individual who, while competent and not acting under duress or undue influence, executed an oath of renunciation but whose death preceded the arrival in CA/OCS/ACS of the paperwork attendant to the oath. In such an instance, the posthumous approval of the CLN would serve to give effect to the intent of the deceased U.S. citizen clearly articulated prior to death.

CA/OCS/ACS would consider approving a CLN in a situation when the deceased U.S. citizen had, prior to or upon completing the standard questionnaire to determine citizenship, advised a consular officer in writing that he/she had or was about to commit an act of expatriation (and the citizen ultimately performed the expatriating act). The communication must indicate unequivocally that the individual was acting voluntarily, fully intending to relinquish his/her U.S. citizenship. Such a written statement to a consular officer indicates that the citizen had reflected upon the consequences attendant to his/her actions and their impact upon his/her citizenship. Therefore, absent any countervailing documentation or other conduct that would put into question the truthfulness or bona fides of the citizen's assertions to the consular officer, a cogent argument in such a case could be made that the preponderance of the evidence reflects the occurrence of loss of citizenship.

On a case-by-case basis, CA/OCS/ACS could consider a request for the issuance of a CLN when an individual who has committed or is on the threshold of committing an act of expatriation has written in a diary, executed an affidavit before someone other than a consular officer, sent a letter to a disinterested third party, etc. that his/her actions in committing the expatriating act were done voluntarily with the intent of relinquishing citizenship. In such cases, the consular officer, in addition to ensuring the bona fides of the written communication, should examine the individual's conduct subsequent to performing the expatriating act in an effort to ascertain whether it was consistent with the written expression of intent.

Finally, since citizenship is a status personal to the individual, absent written documentation from the deceased, CA/OCS/ACS would find it extremely difficult to approve a CLN predicated solely upon the statements of third parties with respect to the intentions of the deceased vis-à-vis his/her U.S. citizenship or with respect to alleged oral statements of the deceased.

7 FAM 1220 APPENDIX G
POSTHUMOUS REVIEW OF LOSS OF U.S.
NATIONALITY

(CT:CON-407: 06-29-2012)

When a finding of loss has already been made (i.e., CA/OCS/ACS (or its predecessor organization) had already approved the CLN) and the late, former U.S. citizen had indicated to the Department in writing (e.g., executed the standard questionnaire to determine citizenship) that he or she had indeed committed the act of expatriation voluntarily with the requisite intent to relinquish, the Office of *Legal Affairs* (*CA/OCS/L*) would be extremely hesitant to recommend reversal of the earlier decision absent compelling evidence that is contemporaneous with the act of expatriation that demonstrates that the deceased's actions were either involuntary or that he/she lacked the intent to relinquish. *CA/OCS/L* generally would not accept self-serving assertions from any possible interested third party. *CA/OCS/L* could, however, consider the documented opinions from disinterested third parties (e.g., mental health professionals, attending physicians) who might be able to shed light upon the state of mind of the individual at the time of the commission of the expatriating act.

When a finding of loss has been made and the Department's files do not reflect in any way that the individual intended to give up U.S. citizenship, CA/OCS would not continue to sustain that finding and *CA/OCS/L* would subsequently vacate the CLN. For example, prior to the U.S. Supreme Court finding in Afroyim, the Department presumed or did not require intent to relinquish citizenship. If a loss of nationality file from this earlier period reflected this decision making, CA/OCS would instead apply current standards for adjudicating loss, which require intent to relinquish citizenship, and may include the administrative presumption that a citizen intends to retain U.S. citizenship under specified circumstances.

When a finding of loss has been made and the statutory basis for the CLN's issuance has been ruled unconstitutional, it would be incumbent upon the Department to posthumously vacate the CLN.

Following the cancellation of the CLN, the Department should, when appropriate, be prepared to approve the consular report of death abroad of a U.S. citizen and issue documentation to any offspring of the deceased American who have or have not been previously documented as U.S. citizens.

CA/OCS/L should advise pertinent federal agencies of the reversal of the finding of loss of nationality in accordance with 7 FAM 1240.

7 FAM 1230 THROUGH 1290 APPENDIX G UNASSIGNED

10

Contact Information

The author is not available for personal consultations. However, you are welcome to share your comments with him. Please note any emails sent may be published on his site and/or used in future articles, books, and/or media.

stateless@glr.com

If you have questions or would like to interact with others that are interested in the topic, Mr. Roberts moderates a web forum entitled "*How to Renounce Your U.S. Citizenship*". The web address is: http://www.howtorenounce.com

You can also view his personal blog / rant at: http://glr.com

The PDF version of this book may be purchased with Bitcoin at: http://www.nimblewisdom.com

Media inquiries can be directed to: mediax@glr.com

www.ingramcontent.com/pod-product-compliance
Lightning Source LLC
Chambersburg PA
CBHW022109280326
41933CB00007B/313